OPPORTUNITIES

in

Event Planning Careers

BLYTHE CAMENSON

VGM Career Books

Chicago   New York   San Francisco   Lisbon   London   Madrid   Mexico City
Milan   New Delhi   San Juan   Seoul   Singapore   Sydney   Toronto

The *McGraw·Hill* Companies

Library of Congress Cataloging-in-Publication Data

Camenson, Blythe.
      Opportunities in event planning careers / Blythe Camenson.
          p.   cm.—(VGM opportunities series)
      Includes bibliographical references.
      ISBN 0-07-138228-3 (paperback)
        1. Special events industry—Vocational guidance.   2. Special events—
Planning. I. Title. II. Series.

GT3405.C35 2002
394.2—dc21   2002069020

1 2 3 4 5 6 7 8 9 0   LBM/LBM   1 0 9 8 7 6 5 4 3 2

ISBN 0-07-138228-3

McGraw-Hill books are available at special quantity discounts to use as premiums and sales promotions, or for use in corporate training programs. For more information, please write to the Director of Special Sales, Professional Publishing, McGraw-Hill, Two Penn Plaza, New York, NY 10121-2298. Or contact your local bookstore.

This book is printed on acid-free paper.

Contents

Foreword

Does event planning sound easy to you? Many people would probably think so, especially if all that came to mind was shopping and cleaning house for a weekend party among friends. Most event planners likely did that, and found that they had a genuine enjoyment not only of the party itself, but also of the process leading up to it.

If they decided to do more party planning and took the next step in becoming a professional in this field, these event planners would wisely seek the training programs and courses available to help them hone their skills. In the course of their training, they might also decide to intern or volunteer their services to gain that all-too-valuable experience in this industry. Now, being intimately involved in all the aspects of planning an event, they begin to understand just how complex, chaotic, thrilling, and, yes, mundane, the profession can be.

Some have likened event planning to the theater—to putting on a production. The event planner (director) is responsible to his or her backers (clients) to make sure that a cast and crew (speakers,

caterers, technicians, etc.) put on the best possible theatrical production (event) for its audience (attendees). Once the curtain goes
up, there is no going back. The production will go on no matter
what happens to jam the works. If Murphy's Law is to be
respected, any and all problems must be anticipated and planned
for. And what about those emergencies that no one could possibly
foresee, you might ask. Well, as a talented event planner, you
would be able to think on your feet and fix any issues that need
to be resolved.

Whatever event you may be called on to plan, it's important
that you put all your energy, patience, attention to minutiae, professionalism, and good humor into the job. What you are creating
means something to someone, be it a bride, corporate employees,
a charity, whatever. You are creating a memorable event—one that
matters—and that is a responsibility that shouldn't be taken lightly.

Opportunities in Event Planning Careers gives you everything
you need to get started. You'll read about which schools offer training and which organizations to contact for help not only in getting
started, but throughout your career as well. You'll find information
that can help you decide if entrepreneur or employee is the best
route for you to take. And the profiles of event planners sprinkled
throughout are a wonderful way to read about what the day-to-day
job is really like.

Are you willing to take on this responsibility? Will you take
advantage of the training and certification available through university programs and industry associations to become the best
event planner possible? Can you look at an event from both a
bird's-eye view and worker ant's perspective in the trenches as you

coordinate all the people and materials involved? Are you a quick thinker who can come up with innovative and effective solutions to problems? If you've answered yes to all of these questions, congratulations. You're well on your way to becoming a successful event planner.

The Editors, VGM Career Books

Acknowledgments

I would like to thank the following professionals for their advice and insight into the world of event planning:

Dianna Bacchi, Event Planner, formerly with McGraw-Hill Publishing, New York, New York

Phyllis Cambria, PartyPlansPlus.com, Event Planner, Author, Coconut Creek, Florida

Stephanie Dooley, Director, Enchantment Events, Albuquerque, New Mexico

Donna Lemire, Bridal Shop Owner, Wedding Planner, Tyngsboro, Massachusetts

Michelle McBain, Convention Services Manager, Crowne Plaza Pyramid Hotel, Albuquerque, New Mexico

Gerard J. Monaghan, President, Association of Bridal
Consultants, New Milford, Connecticut
Doris Nixon, President of Weddings Beautiful
Worldwide, Richmond, Virginia
Mary Tribble, Tribble Creative Group, Event Planner,
Charlotte, North Carolina

1

OVERVIEW OF THE FIELD

EVENT PLANNING IS a broad term that describes a wide open, growing field and encompasses a range of possible employment opportunities. It's also a relatively new field. Event planning, like many other professional fields, came about to fill a need. Whenever people gather, someone has to be in charge of organizing the gathering. Before event planning became a professional field, harried brides and their mothers organized weddings by themselves. Corporate workers lost time from their day-to-day projects to arrange conventions and conferences. Nonprofit workers did the same. Government workers had to leave their assigned duties to take on the added responsibility of planning recruitment fairs or educational events. Whenever a gathering was planned, someone whose job description did not include planning became, by default, the planner.

Hotels and convention centers were most likely the first to see the need for employees with the specific job title of "event planner." As time passed, the need was recognized more widely and professional associations started forming. The purpose of any professional association is to provide recognition for its members, continuing education and certification, and often employment opportunities. Once a field has a professional organization it can be considered a "real" field.

The oldest professional association in the event planning field is the National Bridal Service (NBS), which incorporates Weddings Beautiful Worldwide, a wedding planning service and certifier of wedding planners. It recently celebrated fifty years in business. The International Festivals & Events Association (IFEA) has been around for only forty-five years. Meeting Professionals International (MPI) just celebrated its twenty-fifth year. The Association of Bridal Consultants was formed as recently as 1981 and the newest, the International Special Events Society (ISES), was founded in 1987.

Compare that to the American Medical Association, which was founded in 1847, or the American Bar Association, founded in 1878, and you see how new the field really is.

A Look at the Numbers

Although a new field, event planning is a comfortably large field. And the larger the field the more plentiful the employment opportunities. Conventions, by definition, include trade shows, meetings, and events. Nationally, the convention industry is a $73 billion industry, ranking number seventeen among all U.S. private sector industries.

Trade shows rank in the top ten marketing approaches used by the nation's top companies, according to a recent study by Business Marketing. Expositions account for 17.3 percent of every marketing dollar spent by companies with sales greater than $50 million. A total of 13,185 exhibitions were held in the United States and Canada last year. According to the census of the exhibition industry by the Center for Exhibition Industry Research (find its address and website listing in Appendix A) there are 12,188 shows in the United States and Canada with at least three thousand square feet of space and a minimum of ten exhibitors. Of those, 11,095 are held in the United States and 1,093 are held in Canada.

CEIR reports that events take place in more than two thousand venues. This is how it breaks down:

hotels	39 percent
convention centers	38 percent
conference/seminar facilities	8 percent
other types of facilities	15 percent

This is important information because these are some of the settings in which event planners work. Additional settings are mentioned later in this chapter.

The convention industry employs more than a million and a half people. This includes employees at hotels, convention and conference centers, and other facilities and covers job titles from caterer to security guard to event planner. Although it's impossible to estimate the number of actual full-time planners, for every event planned it's likely that at least one full-time person was involved with the planning. If, as mentioned earlier, this industry held more than thirteen thousand trade shows, a good number of event planners were working to make them happen.

For any potential event planner considering entering this field, the above numbers confirm the old expression that there is safety in numbers. Recorded statistics show a healthy field. And there are countless private parties and events arranged by event planners that the statistics could never cover. In short, the job outlook is good, especially for self-employed entrepreneurs with the ability and drive to drum up business.

What Event Planners Do

Simply put, event planners plan events. They are responsible for every aspect of an event, from setting the date and location, to advertising for attendees, to providing refreshments and arranging for speakers.

Different types of events require the event planner to perform many of the same duties, but also many different ones. Let's look at the type of events they plan and some of what's involved with each:

Types of Events

• *Art show event planners* set the date and location and arrange for the hanging of the artwork and/or display of other items. They send out invitations, provide advertising, and arrange for refreshments.

• *Charity ball and fund-raiser event planners* often must work with the particular charity to plan the theme of the event. They arrange for invitations and mailings, choose the best location, and hire caterers.

• *Concert promoters/planners* hire the performers, announce the fees, set the venue and dates, and arrange for advertising and ticket sales. They often must also provide security and transportation.

• *Convention planners* assign booth space, work with the client to set the schedule for events, hire speakers, set up rooms, make hotel arrangements, and provide catering services.

• *Conference planners* do work similar to that of convention planners; however, while convention planners work for a convention hall, more often than not, conference planners are clients who must establish a liaison with the convention facility. They handle every aspect of the conference, from room assignment and setup to hiring speakers and preparing advertising materials.

• Corporations can employ their own *in-house planners* or hire outside freelancers. The event planner is responsible for every aspect of the event, including setting the location, arranging for audiovisual equipment as needed, and hiring catering services.

• *Exposition, fair, and festival planning* is similar to convention planning and involves many of the same duties, including assigning booth or exhibition space. Exposition planners, as all planners, must consider the number of people they expect to attend and address issues of parking and security.

• *Seminar and workshop education planners* perform the same functions as other event planners including reserving meeting space, arranging for catering, hiring speakers, and advertising the event.

• *Social function planners* work on a range of events such as anniversary parties, birthday parties, Christmas parties and/or other holiday functions, bat/bar mitzvahs, graduation parties, engagement parties, and weddings. Planners of these functions must choose the venue, decide themes and color schemes, order flowers, arrange for catering, and have invitations printed and sent out.

Where Event Planners Work

Event planners work for advertising agencies, hotels, caterers, convention centers, bridal businesses, the government, private corporations, and nonprofit organizations. They are also self-employed, hired by any organization or individual in need of professional organizational skills.

In addition to planning events for hire, some entrepreneurs become event planners to operate their own enterprises—from writers to plumbers to chiropractors. They organize seminars and workshops and conferences for almost every type of professional and recreational interest. These events provide professionals with the means to stay in touch with colleagues and further their skills. They also serve those with specific interests such as financial planning, collecting antiques, writing for publications, learning how to quit smoking or improve health, and enhancing relationships.

Required Skills and Abilities

People with good organizational skills, an ability to attend to detail, and an ability to work under pressure can find rewarding career opportunities creating and staging their own events or those requisitioned by others.

In addition to good organizational skills, someone with a creative spirit, a flair for the dramatic, a sense of adventure, and a love of spectacle could expect to flourish in this field. The specific skills and requirements will depend on the type of job and the training program pursued. Sprinkled throughout this book are sample job listings that highlight the required skills and characteristics. These include:

- computer skills
- willingness to travel
- willingness to work a flexible schedule with long hours
- experience in delegating
- negotiating skills
- verbal and written communication skills
- enthusiasm
- project management skills
- ability to work with high-level executives
- ability to handle multiple tasks simultaneously
- ability to interact with sales and/or catering departments and other vendors
- follow-through skills
- budgeting skills
- being a self-starter
- ability to initiate and close sales
- familiarity with audiovisual equipment
- lots of patience

Event planning can be incredibly time consuming. A good event planner must be a juggler, especially if business takes off and you have more than one event to plan at a time. It's hard enough balancing all of the elements of one event. Imagine if there are two or three—or even more—events going on at the same time. The more events you have to plan, the more staff you'll need. This is what makes a business grow, but it's also what can add to the stress and headaches of the job. Now, the event planner is not only planning events, but he or she also has to manage an office and employees. How will you acquire the skills and abilities you'll need? The professional associations described later in this chapter provide rigorous training and licensing procedures. In addition, a few universities are starting to offer degrees in the field. The training programs available and the certification processes are covered in Chapter 2.

There are also career-specific publications, including *Special Events Magazine* and *FESTIVALS: The How-To of Festivals & Events*, that help keep professional event planners up to date in their field. Appendix B lists these magazines, as well as other resources, and how to locate them.

Building Your Résumé

For those just starting out, trying to get a career in event planning off the ground is difficult to do without any experience. But, just maybe, you have more experience than you realize. Have you been organizing family birthday parties? Did you get a baby-sitting service started as a kid? How about camp? Did you plan a photography contest or help set up team events? And in college, did you organize sorority luncheons or garden parties? All of this translates to skills and experience directly relevant to a career in event planning.

To gain additional experience, seek out internships, either through your college or the professional associations covered later in this chapter.

Possible Job Titles

Because this new career can be found in a range of industries—from private corporations and nonprofits to the government sector—job titles will vary accordingly. Many of the job titles listed below are given to people who perform the same duties. Often the job setting and industry determines the job title. In addition to those listed here, there are many more varieties possible.

- Account Manager
- Bridal Consultant
- Conference Center Services Representative
- Conference Coordinator
- Conference Manager
- Conference Planner
- Convention Coordinator
- Customer Events Planner
- Event Coordinator
- Event Planner
- Meeting Coordinator
- Meeting Director
- Meeting and Exhibits Director
- Meeting Manager
- Meeting Planner
- Program Coordinator
- Public Affairs Coordinator
- Sales Manager
- Trade Show Director

Steps to Successful Event Planning

Part of landing that first contract involves putting together a proposal for the client. The proposal would include everything from the type of venue to the decorations. To complete the proposal, the event planner must speak to vendors and lock down costs for such things as flowers or musicians, depending on what's needed for the specific event.

Once the contract with the client is signed a number of things happen. The planner must sign contracts with the vendors. Depending on the event and the requirements, these vendors can include some or all of the following:

- caterers
- rental companies
- decor designers
- lighting companies
- tent suppliers
- entertainers
- site venue
- printers
- promotional specialties
- floral designers
- plant rentals
- hospitality staffing
- photographers and videographers
- transportation suppliers
- communication systems
- signage
- security

Be prepared to have several meetings and consultations with the client. During the course of the planning, there are usually changes the client would need to agree to.

Planners who are well organized usually create an overall time-line for the entire event, from the beginning of planning to the event day and beyond for any follow-up. The schedule could encompass day-by-day activities in preparation for the big day. When putting together the timeline, you would need to be aware of how schedules must work. For instance, if you want to have spotlights on certain tables, you'll have to wait until the tables are placed to set the spotlights up. You could also create an additional timeline for the setup before the event, activities during the event, and how the tear-down will proceed. All timelines and schedules are distributed to the involved parties.

You would need to prepare a complete contact sheet so each vendor and key personnel can easily reach one another. This would include beeper numbers, cell phones, papers, home phones, faxes, and E-mail addresses.

As the date of the event draws nearer, it's usual practice to schedule an operations meeting at the venue. This would include all those involved in the event to do a walk-through or rehearsal so everyone is aware of any final changes and everyone is working from the same schedule.

Earnings for Event Planners

As within any industry, salaries differ greatly depending on the type of employer, the employer's budget, and the region of the country. A self-employed entrepreneur could make more money than someone working for a hotel would, for example, but it might take several years for the advanced salary figures to start kicking in.

It is not possible to say which category of event planners earns the most. A charity fund-raiser working for a nonprofit could earn more than a corporate for-profit planner, if the salary is straight commission based on the amount raised, for example. One self-employed planner could earn in the millions, while another would earn very little because she or he doesn't do the work necessary to find business.

Planners working for a salary plus commission or for a straight commission would expect their salaries to be based, at least in part, on how much effort they put into drumming up business. Any event planner on a commission basis, whether working for a nonprofit organization, the government, or the private sector, can expect earnings that reflect to a large degree the amount of effort he or she expends. Particular to this field, a planner is more often than not rewarded on the success of the event and the number of events the planner organizes. In general, planners working fulltime earn a fairly decent income.

Corporate Event Planners

Meetings & Conventions magazine commissioned a survey of corporate event planners. The survey was conducted by The Survey Center, an independent market-research company based in Massachusetts. The center polled eight hundred corporate meeting planners in the United States, chosen randomly from the magazine's subscriber database. The planners were asked about their compensation, benefits, job satisfaction, and work habits.

The survey revealed the following:

- About 91 percent of the planners surveyed reported they are satisfied with their jobs. They believe they are well paid and they are content.
- The average annual base salary three years ago was slightly more than $60,000.

- Approximately 20 percent had a base salary of more than $80,000.
- About 49 percent made between $30,000 and $59,999.
- There were 5 percent who made an annual salary of $150,000 or more.
- Men made an average of $27,719 more than women did. The men averaged $76,079; women averaged $48,360.
- About 12 percent made less than $29,999.
- One-third of those surveyed received cash bonuses.
- Close to 75 percent were satisfied with their income level.
- Some 92 percent were not worried about being laid off in the near future.
- Approximately one-third of the planners who responded expected to add employees to their events departments in the next twelve months.
- Salaries increased as planners got older. Those younger than 35 earned an average of $44,938; those 35 to 54 made $60,942; and planners 55 and older averaged $73,952.
- Salaries also increased depending upon job title and responsibilities. Corporate executives and managers earned $82,258; those with titles specific to meetings, such as "meeting planner" or "convention manager," had an average salary of $50,708. Those in general management or administration earned $50,206, and planners with titles falling into the "other" category took home $55,588.

The survey also showed regional differences. Chicago is the best place to work as a corporate planner. There the average salary is

$67,331, about $3,500 more than in the northeast or western states. The Pacific region came in second, with $63,883 as an average yearly salary, and the Northeast came in third at $63,827.

The mountain region was ranked at fourth, with an annual average salary of $59,298. Next came the central South at $56,518. Following that came the South Atlantic with $54,925; then at the bottom of the list, the western north-central brought up at $49,963. The population size and cost of living and standard salary ranges traditional in these areas most likely account for the variations in earnings across the country.

Meeting Managers

According to the 2002–2003 *Occupational Outlook Handbook*, hotel-based sales and meeting managers earned a median annual income in the year 2000 of $42,210. According to Yahoo.com's "salary wizard" reports, convention and meeting managers working in the United States in all settings earn a median base salary of $43,734. The top half of earners are paid an average of $52,779. The lower half of earners are paid an average of $35,466.

Wedding Planners

Wedding planners can work for a percentage of the bride's wedding budget; for an hourly rate of $40 to $100, depending upon the region of the country; or for a flat fee. Annual salaries vary greatly from wedding planner to wedding planner. Someone just starting out would logically expect to earn much less than someone who's been in the business for a while and gets a good number of clients. (See Chapter 4.)

Gerard Monaghan, president of the Association of Bridal Consultants says, "We just published a survey of members. While not scientifically accurate, it does give a hint of the numbers. Members report their income as averaging $42,795. The typical wedding they handle is about $28,800." Wedding planners who charge a percentage of a wedding budget would average approximately $2,880 to $4,320 per wedding.

How much experience the planner has often will determine the rate of pay. Mary Tribble of Tribble Creative Group, an event planning and production company, reveals how her company sets its fees:

> Principal rates (that's for my partner and myself . . . she has 20 years experience; I have 17 years) bill at $125 an hour. My event managers (ranging from 8 to 20 years experience) bill at $75, and my event coordinators with 2 to 8 years experience, bill at $55. Annually, a self-employed freelance planner could earn anywhere from $35,000 to $75,000. Maybe more if they are in a good market and have an incredible reputation.
>
> Fees for our projects can range from $5,000 to $50,000 or more, depending on the complexity of the project. But it would be unlikely for a one-person freelancer to be able to command a $50,000 project fee. When we charge that much, the client is getting a whole team of people (principals, event managers, coordinators, and marketing specialists) to produce their event.

Sample Job Listings

Here and throughout the book relevant actual sample job listings are provided to give you an idea of the type of jobs available. Because the listings are meant as samples only, the hiring firms and contact people are not mentioned. You can locate similar listings by searching the Internet using keywords such as "event planning," "jobs," "careers," and so on.

Many of the professional associations featured throughout this book maintain job banks at their websites. Members are given passwords to access these areas, where related jobs, and sometimes internships, are listed. Websites are provided in Appendix A.

Job Title: Meeting Planner

Type of Organization: Trade association

Location: New York City

Position Description: Major trade association headquartered in New York City seeks a meeting professional. Works closely with program committees to develop and manage five to six local, regional, and national meetings annually, ranging in size from three hundred to fifteen hundred attendees. Responsibilities include hotel/site selection, negotiating contracts, determining audiovisual requirements, managing multiple speakers, preparing and supervising budgets, overseeing print production of promotional brochures, and writing copy for collateral material.

Qualifications and Experience: Experience with trade shows management is an asset. Needs to travel approximately 15 percent of the time. Requires good problem-solving and communication skills, strong organizational skills, and ability to multitask. Must be able to operate as a team player and at the same time work independently in a satellite office. Minimum of two to five years of meeting planning experience, preferably in an association setting.

Salary: $45,000 to $50,000 plus excellent benefits.

Job Title: *Conference Manager*

Type of Organization: Nonprofit history-related professional association

Location: Washington, D.C.

Position Description: National nonprofit seeks professional meeting planner to manage all aspects of an annual conference for 2,000+ people, including educational programs, field sessions, and social events.

Qualifications and Experience: Requirements include three to five years of administration, marketing, and conference planning experience, preferably with culturally related programs. Strong financial management skills and ability to manage multiple priorities and deadlines a must.

Salary: $45,000 to $59,999.

Contact Information: Curriculum vitae and cover letter via regular post.

Job Title: *Executive Director*

Type of Organization: Arts festival

Location: Tennessee

Position Description: Growing festival organization has an annual budget exceeding $500,000 and a staff of three employees. Seeking an executive director to manage all activities associated with the festival's mission, including an "Arts in the Park" festival.

Qualifications and Experience: Ability to attract sponsors and volunteers, provide leadership and direction, and develop innovative enhancements for growth are necessary. Knowledge of sponsorship solicitation, festival management, cost control, and artistic outreach programs is required.

Salary: $35,000 to $44,999.

Contact Information: Résumé with salary requirements via fax, E-mail, or regular mail.

Professional Associations for Event Planners

In the field of event planning, professional associations play a large role in contributing to the professional development of individual members and their employing companies. Through professional associations, event planners can receive training and prestigious certification. They can network with other professionals and be put in contact with vendors providing related services or products.

For those interested in self-employment, professional associations can help with a business plan and provide near round-the-clock consultation services. Have a question? Not sure what to do? There'll be an expert available to help you.

Some associations maintain job banks or provide referral services. The association websites are not just for the members; they're for potential clients as well. Most maintain a bookstore or library with helpful event planning reference material. Some also publish magazines or newsletters.

The three main professional associations for event planners follow. They cater to generalist event planners—that is, planners who tend not to specialize—and produce a variety of events.

Because weddings are such a specialized field, the professional associations for that area are featured separately in Chapter 4. Contact information for the organizations highlighted here is provided in Appendix A.

International Festivals & Events Association (IFEA)

IFEA provides a forum for event managers from around the world to network and exchange ideas. More than twenty-seven hundred professionals are currently members of the International Festivals & Events Association, which covers a broad spectrum of organizations. The International Festivals & Events Association has provided cutting-edge professional development and fund-raising ideas to the special events industry for forty-five years. Through publications, seminars, the annual convention and trade show, and ongoing networking, IFEA is advancing festivals and events throughout the world. IFEA members gain ideas on how other festivals excel in sponsorship, marketing, fund-raising, operations, volunteer coordination, management, and much more.

Events include:

- large events
- small events
- arts festivals
- sporting events
- fairs
- parks and recreation activities
- city offices events

- convention and visitors bureaus activities
- chambers of commerce events

IFEA membership ranges from the Kentucky Derby Festival and Pasadena Tournament of Roses Parade to the Taste of Chicago and the Barbecue Goat Cook-Off in Brady, Texas. Included also are the Macy's Thanksgiving Day Parade and the Cardboard Boat Races in Heber Springs, Arkansas.

Any organization involved in the planning of events and festivals, tourism promotion, and sponsorship benefits from membership in the IFEA. The IFEA also produces an annual convention and trade show, where hundreds of the world's event managers come together to share information on every aspect of event planning through workshops, roundtable discussions, and networking. For convention and trade show locations, consult the IFEA website listed in Appendix A.

If you or your company decide to become a member of the IFEA, you will be eligible to receive the following membership benefits:

- *Free member consulting service.* Members have access to other members who are more experienced or are experts in the field. These experts provide a valuable resource and are available to help with particular problems event planners might be having.

- *The IFEA Job Bank.* The job bank lists available jobs around the world. The number of jobs listed varies and is updated on a regular basis.

- *Internships.* Students can find internships to complete their educational program requirements and gain valuable experience.

• *Member recognition.* If you have been accepted as a member, you're able to display the IFEA designation and be recognized as a professional.

In addition, the IFEA offers the CFE—Certified Festival Executive program. This is one of the certifying programs for event planners and is covered in detail in Chapter 2.

Members also receive a free subscription to the IFEA magazine, *FESTIVALS: The How-To of Festivals & Events.* Membership fees are based on the new member's company budget, and students may join at a discounted rate.

International Special Events Society (ISES)

Founded in 1987, the International Special Events Society (ISES) now has nearly three thousand members active in thirty chapters throughout the world. The ISES mission is to foster "enlightened performance through education while promoting ethical conduct."

To that end, the society strives to uphold the integrity of the special events profession to the general public through its code of ethics. It also acquires and disseminates useful business information to members. The society fosters a spirit of cooperation among members and other special events professionals and attempts to cultivate high standards of business practices.

ISES members, among others, include:

• caterers
• meeting planners
• decorators
• event planners

- audiovisual technicians
- party and convention coordinators
- educators
- journalists
- hotel sales managers

ISES member benefits include scholarships and funding for education and research, a bookstore, an online message board so members can communicate with each other, a subscription to *SpecialEvents* magazine, and a speaker database to help planners find appropriate guests for their events. ISES also offers continuing education and another event planning certification—the Certified Special Events Professional (CSEP) designation. (This is covered in detail in Chapter 2.)

For information on membership categories and fees, or to download a membership application, log on to the following: ises.com/membership/ISES_membership_application.pdf.

Meeting Professionals International (MPI)

Meeting Professionals International (MPI), which was founded in the late 1970s, states in its vision statement that it is committed to shaping and defining the future of the meeting and event industry. "With more than 19,000 members in 64 countries, 60 chapters and 4 chapters in formation, MPI empowers its members with personal and professional excellence by providing them with superior education, research, professional development and networking opportunities."

MPI member benefits include professional development and networking opportunities through international conferences, customized education events, and chapter meetings. MPI also maintains an extensive online job bank and allows members to list their résumés. As do the other organizations, MPI provides an online bookstore. Publications available from all the event planning professional associations are listed in Appendix B. Members receive a free subscription to *The Meeting Professional*.

MPI also offers its own certification programs, conferring the Certification in Meeting Management (CMM) and Certified Meeting Professional (CMP). These certification programs are covered in detail in Chapter 2.

MPI membership dues are paid annually for individual members. Check with MPI to verify current dues. You can find their online application at: mpiweb.org/members/membership/app.asp.

Additional Help

The Center for Exhibition Industry Research (CEIR) conducts research designed to help planners master the science of exhibition marketing. Corporate exhibit managers, exhibition designers and brokers, contractors and suppliers, association managers, exhibition organizers, advertising and consulting firms, and hotel and facility managers use its marketing and research reports.

CEIR's reports focus on how professionals can maximize their marketing effectiveness. They produce new reports every other month. These reports cover topics such as:

- The Power of Exhibitions—The value of exhibitions in the purchasing cycle is discussed.
- Marketing/Communications—Strategies for effective trade show and exhibit marketing are offered.

- Sales/Measuring Return—Specific exhibition-related objectives are analyzed and compared to other marketing media.

Attendee/exhibitor characteristics include the following:

- International—Methods to attract international exhibitors and attendees to U.S. shows are highlighted.
- Industry Trends—Exhibition industry growth projections are given.
- Facts and Figures—Data from throughout the industry are examined.
- Special Reports Series—CEIR reports are available for a fee and can be ordered online at ceir.org.

Joining a professional association and seeking expert help can be a good career move. However, it's not necessary to join right away. In fact, some associations expect members to have accrued a number of years of experience before they're eligible to join.

Those just starting out can attend professional association functions. Most associations will allow newcomers to attend meetings and will charge only slightly higher fees than a member is charged. These meetings and conferences are essential to your education and growth.

Evaluate the benefits each association has to offer; talk to members, whom you can find through the websites; and see which organization memberships would suit your needs and career goals. The field is exciting and ever evolving, and the professional associations play a large role in helping their members maintain a high standard of professionalism. The more professional the event planner, the more successful he or she will be.

2

PREPARING YOURSELF FOR A
CAREER IN EVENT PLANNING

BECAUSE EVENT PLANNING is a fairly new discipline, twenty years or so ago there were no real formal training programs. Event planners performed their duties on a wing and a prayer, so to speak, and learned by trial and error as they went.

Phyllis Cambria, who is co-author with Patty Sachs of *The Complete Idiot's Guide to Throwing a Great Party* and co-owner of PartyPlansPlus.com says, "Like many long-time event planners, there wasn't a course of study offered when we got started. In fact, there wasn't much of an event industry, per se, so I 'backed-into' the industry. Much of my initial training was on the job."

These days there are ways to get trained and certified as an event planner, but the options are not as broad as for other careers. There are just a few universities that offer degree programs. Some focus on undergraduate degrees and others offer graduate programs. Learning can take place in a classroom or, with the advent of online learning, from the comfort of a home office. Also, the professional associations in this field play a large role in training and certifying event planners. Each association administers its own certification program.

Even those individuals who have been in the business a long time and have been self-taught have gone after a variety of certifications to give themselves more knowledge and credibility in the field.

"Over the years, I have taken courses given through the International Special Events Society," says Phyllis Cambria. Although the process of earning certification is not an easy one, she says, "it pays off in two ways: respect from your peers and your standing in the event community is raised; and you can use it as a marketing tool for clients, who will usually be fairly impressed when you tell them what the CSEP designation means."

The International Special Events Society's CSEP (Certified Special Events Professional) certification is just one of several available. These are covered in detail in this chapter, along with five university programs currently available. No doubt in the years to come more and more programs will be added to the roster. Make sure to check the college guides to see which schools might have added an event planning program or department.

If traveling to a city where one of the university programs featured here is offered is not possible, there are alternatives. Many universities across the country offer courses and programs in the related fields of hotel management, hospitality, and recreation. Talk to the department advisor at your university of choice to see how well suited its related program would be to your career goals.

Program fees vary greatly from one institution to another. Check with each program or visit each website to verify course costs.

University Programs

Five universities offering event planning programs are featured here. They are George Washington University, the University of Minnesota, the University of Illinois at Urbana-Champaign, Purdue University, and the University of Nevada at Las Vegas.

George Washington University

George Washington University offers event management certificates and degree programs in event planning.

Event Management Certificate and Degree Programs

George Washington University offers a Professional Certificate in Event Management through the Department of Tourism and Hospitality Management in the School of Business and Public Management. Students have three choices how to study for and earn this certificate:

1. Distance Learning. If you have a computer, distance learning lets you earn a certificate from your home or office or even while traveling. You will receive a password that will gain you entry to the GW Event Management distance learning Internet site, with access to the same materials provided during classroom instruction, plus online slides and audio lectures. You can also chat online with other students and professors and complete the course quizzes, receiving instant feedback.

The George Washington University Event Management Program via Distance Learning is designed to accommodate busy schedules. The core courses are conducted online using Prometheus, a Web-based courseware application, and supported by a textbook, workbook, and audio Power Point presentation.

The George Washington University's Event Management Certificate Program is a comprehensive professional development program.

As Alice Conway, Director, GWU Event Management Certificate Program, says, "It offers education designed for beginning as well as experienced event managers. Our extensive experience teaching in the classroom—and practicing the event management discipline—has enabled us to continually improve the content by modifying and expanding courses to meet the ever-changing needs of those in the field. The distance learning program, which has been expanded, allows you to take courses at your own pace using printed materials, videos, and the Internet. If you are already following the traditional classroom format, you have the option of switching to distance learning if you desire."

2. *Weekend Courses.* With this option students can complete all courses in seven months.

Courses meet on Fridays from 5:30 P.M. to 9:30 P.M. and on Saturdays from 9:00 A.M. to 6:00 P.M.

3. *Weekday/Accelerated Courses.* With this option students can complete all courses in three weeks. Each course meets for two days from 9:00 A.M. to 4:00 P.M. The program is held three times per year.

Students are also allowed to mix and match the weekend format with distance learning and weekday courses to complete the program within a convenient time frame.

How to Earn the GW Certificate in Event Management

To earn the certificate in Event Management from the George Washington University School of Business and Public Management, students must complete the following:

- four core courses and three electives
- seventy-five hours of practicum
- a professional portfolio that documents an actual event you have managed or helped coordinate
- a comprehensive exam of one hundred multiple choice questions and an essay covering material from the four core courses.

Courses

Best Practices in Event Management

Event Coordination

Event Marketing

Risk Management: Financial, Legal, and Ethical
    Safeguards

CAP: Career Advancement Program

Catering Design and Coordination

Corporate Event Management

Event Fund-Raising

Introduction to Event Information Systems (EIS)

Event Laboratory

Event Management Motivational Seminar

Event Sponsorship

Exposition/Trade Show Planning Management and
    Marketing

Government, Civic, and Political Events

Meetings and Conferences

Sport Event Marketing and Management

Starting, Growing, and Managing an Event Business

Wedding Planning, Coordination, and Consulting

Internet Event Marketing

Celebrating Historical Events

Work Toward the CSEP

The GWU program helps students prepare for the International Special Events Society's Certified Special Events Professional (CSEP) designation. (See information on the CSEP later in this chapter.) The ISES awards a maximum of ten continuing event management education (CEME) points through GWU to help students earn the CSEP designation.

Who Should Enroll in This Program?

This program would be well suited to those already working in the field, whether as an administrative assistant or entrepreneur, if your professional responsibilities include coordinating meetings, conferences, expositions, social programs, reunions, and sports or other types of events.

Or, if you're just starting out, looking for an entry-level position, or seeking a career change, this program can benefit you, too. Often people employed in related fields, such as lighting, sound, audiovisual, decor, catering, and entertainment, decide to switch gears and enter this program to help them do so.

Degree Programs

George Washington University offers the Bachelor's of Business Administration with a field specialization in tourism and hospitality management. This would be sufficient for most individuals either new or already familiar to the field.

For those seeking job advancement and promotion, or for those who already have a bachelor's degree in another subject and might not want to go for another B.A., pursuing a master's degree might be the answer. The university also offers three graduate degrees:

1. Master's of Business Administration (M.B.A.)
2. Master's of Tourism Administration (M.T.A.)
3. Doctor of Philosophy (Ph.D.)

The master's degree programs can be earned through distance education.

Career Opportunities

Graduates of GWU programs have gone on to prestigious positions, including event manager at the Smithsonian Institution, director of public relations for the City of Falls Church, Virginia, protocol office for the State Department, event manager for the Supreme Court, and more.

George Washington University event management students receive a password to a GWU website that lists dozens of event management job leads and internships throughout the world. Students can also benefit from career counseling services provided by the School of Business and Public Management Graduate Career Center.

Applications

GWU applications are available for download by going to gwutourism.org/main.html or by contacting the university directly. The address of the Department of Tourism and Hospitality Management is listed in Appendix C.

University of Minnesota Extension Service

The University of Minnesota Extension Service, through its Tourism Center, has designed a Certified Festival Management Program that focuses on community event planning.

Certified Festival Management Program

Students learn the impact event marketing makes on communities and develop a better understanding of the interaction among the city officials, chambers of commerce, and the community at large.

Students can participate in the program either in person or online. The program is delivered in three levels. Level one is a three-day, eighteen-hour introductory program covering the following courses:

Leadership and Volunteer Management
Planning and Organization
Crisis and Risk Management
Financial Management and Sponsorship
Marketing and Promotion

Level two is a three-day, eighteen-hour course that expands on the topics covered in level one. Level three is a three-hour workshop that concentrates on a different industry topic each year. (The topic for fall of 2002 was "Creating an Integrated Marketing Campaign.")

Certification

Completion of course requirements leads to certification by the Minnesota Festival and Events Association (MFEA). Requirements include: completion of all three courses, attendance at one MFEA conference within two years, and analyzing another event, either produced by the student or by someone else.

Completing this course is one of the options that will lead candidates toward the Certified Festival Executive (CFE) designation, which is awarded by the International Festivals & Events Association (IFEA). You will find more detailed information on the CFE later in this chapter.

You can learn more about the University of Minnesota program by visiting its website at tourism.umn.edu or by contacting it at the address provided in Appendix C.

University of Illinois at Urbana-Champaign

The leisure industry ranks as one of the top three industries in almost every state and generates more than $300 billion nationwide. The University of Illinois's leisure studies program ranks among the top three in the field. Leisure studies covers a wide range of disciplines, including special event or facility management.

Department of Leisure Studies Degree Programs

The University of Illinois at Urbana-Champaign, Department of Leisure Studies, offers an undergraduate degree and two graduate degrees: a Master of Science (M.S.) and a Doctor of Philosophy (Ph.D.).

Internships

Students at both the undergraduate and graduate levels participate in a semester-long internship that provides the opportunity to use the knowledge and skills learned in classes in a professional setting. Internships often help with contacts that can lead to job placement after graduation.

You can learn more about the University of Illinois at Urbana-Champaign program by visiting its website at leisurestudies .uiuc.edu or by contacting it at the address provided in Appendix C.

Purdue University

Purdue University's Hospitality and Tourism Management Department offers a degree in hospitality and tourism management and course work toward the CFE designation (see information on the CFE later in this chapter). This degree opens up many career possibilities, including working in a hotel, resort, or casino; managing a restaurant; running a local tourism bureau; or planning large conventions, banquets, or wedding receptions.

Restaurant Hotel Institutional and Tourism Management Degree Programs

Purdue offers an undergraduate degree and an M.S. degree. Course work and internships are integral parts of each program. You can learn more about Purdue University's program by visiting its website at cfs.purdue.edu/RHIT or by contacting it at the address provided in Appendix C.

University of Nevada at Las Vegas Tourism and Convention Administration Department

What better place to study about the entertainment industry and about convention, meeting, and event planning than in Las Vegas? Las Vegas is known as the entertainment capital of the world. In addition to its more than 120,000 hotel rooms and eleven of the thirteen largest hotels in the world, Las Vegas is also the home to major conventions and trade shows, too.

Programs

1. Bachelor of Science in Hotel Administration with concentrations available in convention/meetings management,

entertainment and event management, casino management, and human resources.

2. Master of Hospitality Administration Executive Program with concentrations (distance learning) available in meetings, events, conventions, and expositions; hospitality marketing; and hospitality accounting and technology.
3. Master of Science in Hotel Administration
4. Ph.D. in Hospitality Administration

Sample Courses
Introduction to the Convention Industry
Catering Sales and Operations
Meeting Planning
Convention Facility Management
Trade Show Operations
Exhibit Management
International Exhibition and Exposition Management
Advanced Meeting Planning
Internship (hands-on practical experience in the convention field)
Sport and Concert Arena Management
Association Management, Special Events Management
Festival and Event Management
Media in Entertainment
Hotel Entertainment
Production Show Management

The Leisure Studies Program, part of the Tourism and Convention Administration Department, offers separate bachelor's and master's degrees.

Learn more about University of Nevada at Las Vegas's program by visiting its website at unlv.edu/tourism or by contacting it at the address provided in Appendix C.

Professional Association Training and Certification Programs

The special events industry has experienced rapid growth over the past several years, and it is changing and evolving at an even faster pace. Today, special events are more challenging and require a higher level of training and experience.

Another very popular route to receive training and certification in event planning is through the professional certification programs the major event planning professional associations offer. Seeking out and earning certification shows clients and colleagues your commitment to the profession. Certification can enhance your professional credibility and provide proof of expertise. Note that most certification programs expect you to have worked in the field for a specific number of years before granting their professional designation.

The following three programs provide information and training for people involved in the many different areas of event planning. Later in this chapter, training and certification programs geared specifically for wedding planners are featured.

International Festivals & Events Association (IFEA) Certified Festival Executive (CFE)

The IFEA's Certified Festival Executive program was founded in 1983 to enhance the level of festival management performance.

The CFE program is offered in conjunction with Purdue University. To date, 649 people have begun or completed the program, and currently there are 130 CFEs.

Those who enroll for the Certified Festival Executive designation have made a commitment to excellence in festival and event management, career advancement, and an ongoing pursuit of knowledge.

CFE Eligibility Requirements

IFEA members and nonmembers beginning the process to attain the CFE designation must meet the following qualifications:

- be executives with four years of paid, full-time, festival-related industry executive and managerial experience
- have attended a minimum of four IFEA conventions within the six years previous to the date of certification. Attendance at any two IFEA regional or state seminars/conventions can substitute for attendance at one or more conventions; however, CFE students must attend a minimum of one IFEA convention to graduate.
- pledge in writing to adhere to the IFEA Code of Standards of Conduct and Ethics
- successfully complete a minimum of four IFEA/Purdue-sponsored courses. (Courses currently offered include Leadership, Personnel Management Creativity, Customer Service, Stress Management, Strategic Planning, Sponsorship/Fund-Raising, and Resource Management.)
- attend the IFEA New Professionals Seminar or attend courses during the convention or at regional/state seminars on financial management, sponsorship, marketing, opera-

tions, administration, and public relations; or complete the University of Minnesota's Certified Festival Management Program, discussed earlier in this chapter
- earn one hundred points by attending specific IFEA seminars, speak at a seminar or convention, or serve on an IFEA committee, board, or council. For full point details visit ifea.com/education/cfe.asp.

According to the IFEA, "The CFE Program is a four-part process based on festival and event management experience, achievements and knowledge. Enrolling in the program and fulfilling the requirements listed above is the first step. Completing the application is next. Successfully completing an oral interview with member(s) of the CFE Commission is the third. After achieving the CFE designation, the fourth step is to maintain the designation through continuing education and participation in the profession [recertification]."

Benefits

Benefits of achieving CFE status include gaining:

- the ability to negotiate a better financial compensation package
- recognition by peers
- knowledge and further insights into the festival industry

For more information on the program, fees, and how to enroll, contact the IFEA or visit its website at ifea.com/education/cfe.asp.

International Special Events Society (ISES) Certified Special Events Professional (CSEP)

The CSEP designation, awarded by the International Special Events Society (ISES) and its certification committee, is considered the hallmark of professional achievement in the special events industry. The ISES states, "It is earned through education, performance, experience, service to the industry, portfolio presentation and examination, and reflects a commitment to professional conduct and ethics."

"The Certified Special Events Professional designation offered by ISES is one of the most complex and rigorous in the industry," says event planning expert and author, Joe Goldblatt. (See Appendix B for a list of his books.) Because of its complex nature, the ISES certification committee and staff help certification candidates through the process by providing:

- orientation programs that explain the requirements, commitment, and other details
- mentors to help candidates through the process
- study materials and a bibliography of suggested reading materials
- study groups

Basic Requirements

Part of the assessment process includes a point system accumulated through experience and service. Candidates for certification begin a self-study program or join a study group. They prepare for the exam and complete the application form, and then sit for the exam. The CSEP exam consists of three parts: (1) essay: a case study in which the exam candidate demonstrates his/her mastery of the required competencies; (2) objective: based on the Glossary of Terms; (3) portfolio assessment.

The exam is offered at the ISES Conference for Professional Development (CPD) in August as well as other times throughout the year. For more details and to download the application, visit the ISES website at ises.com.

Study Materials

Upon enrollment in the CSEP program you will receive a self-study guide, a resource list, and a form to help indicate points accumulated and other vital information. The optional study group course is based on an eight-week outline. Candidates are also put in touch with mentors and trainers and given a workbook with practice exercises and review.

For course fees and enrollment information, visit the ISES website at ises.com.

Meeting Professionals International (MPI)

MPI offers professional development through online learning programs, publications, educational seminars, and conferences and through its two certification programs: the Certified Meeting Professional (CMP) and Certification in Meeting Management (CMM).

Meeting Professionals International considers its CMP designation to be tactical in nature. The CMM is structured to complement the CMP designation and focuses on strategic initiatives and executive decision making.

Certified Meeting Professional (CMP)

Event planners who achieve the CMP designation can benefit in the following ways:

- They receive permission to use the CMP designation after their name and on letterhead, business cards, and other printed matter.
- They receive a certificate suitable for framing and free subscriptions from the Convention Industry Council (CIC) to two newsletters: *The CMP Update* and *The CMP Newsletter*.
- They receive recognition, their name will be released to the press, and their employers will be notified.
- They receive increased knowledge of all aspects of meeting management.
- They can expect to receive an increase in income. Studies show CMPs earn up to $10,000 more annually than non-CMPs.

Candidates should have at least three years of event planning experience, and be currently employed in event planning with responsibility for the successful completion of events or meetings.

To get a CMP application kit, send a $35 check payable to Convention Industry Council to the address below. Be sure to also include your name, title, company/organization, address, city, state/province, country, ZIP/postal code, and phone/fax numbers:

Convention Industry Council (CIC)
8201 Greensboro Drive, Suite 300
McLean, VA 22102
(703) 610-9030
Fax: (703) 610-900

According to the MPI, CMP applications are evaluated by the CMP Board and are based on a point system. Points are awarded for meeting management experience, responsibilities, and education. Additional points are accrued by having membership(s) in professional meeting management organizations and making contributions to the profession. The application can be self-scored for assessment of sufficient points.

The CMP examination takes three hours and consists of 150 multiple choice questions covering the functions a meeting professional must perform. These functions are listed in the CMP application.

Certification in Meeting Management (CMM)

The MPI Certification in Meeting Management (CMM) is geared toward senior-level meeting professionals and affords the opportunity for:

- education in strategic planning and acting
- global certification, prestige, and industry recognition
- potential career advancement
- a networking community of other senior-level people

The program has four aspects:

Pre-Residency: This includes active participation in an MPI learning group using technology, and various reading assignments.

Residency: This requires attendance at an intense four-and-a-half-day residency program in a campuslike atmosphere with participation in a group case study and individual examination.

Exam: The exam is open-book and open-notes. The exam is composed of essay questions and asks you to apply what you learned to your own organization/situation.

Post-Residency: This involves the completion of a post-residency business project.

The CMM designation is obtained through a numerical scoring process of the above parts. According to MPI's policy, scores are not revealed, even to the attendee. Candidates either attain the CMM or are "working toward attainment." Candidates can have more than one chance to reach the designation.

For enrollment fees and additional course information, visit the MPI website at mpi.com. Study and reference materials are available at an additional cost through the MPI bookstore. Call (972) 702-3044 or visit the online bookstore.

A limited number of scholarships are available to individuals who can demonstrate a financial need.

Training Programs for Wedding Planners

Although the above mentioned programs all provide good solid training in various aspects of event planning, including wedding planning, the wedding industry offers its own tailor-made training programs. The Association of Bridal Consultants and Weddings Beautiful Worldwide, a division of the National Bridal Service (NBS), provide these two programs.

Association of Bridal Consultants

The Association of Bridal Consultants is a membership service organization designed to increase awareness of the wedding business and improve the professionalism of its members. This means that someone completing these programs will be a trained professional of the highest standard. (We will examine the work of wedding planners in detail in Chapter 4.)

One of the benefits of membership in the association is its Professional Development Program. The program offers three levels of achievement with certificates awarded at each level. The terms for the three levels are trademarked and each level requires more effort as students work through the program. Once students earn a designation, they can use it in their promotional materials to set themselves apart from the competition.

The levels and their requirements are:

Professional Bridal Consultant

To achieve this designation students must complete a five-course home-study program. The program allows for the courses to be completed in any order. Association of Bridal Consultants members in good standing have no time limit to complete the program. As published in the association's online catalog (bridalassn.com), courses for the Professional Bridal Consultant level include:

Etiquette: Planning the "perfect" wedding, including invitations, announcements, parties, gifts, and a special section on second weddings.

Sales and Marketing: The business side of being a consultant, including marketing, advertising, media relations, company organization, and finances.

Wedding Day: The ceremony and reception, including seating arrangements, protocol, catering, rentals, at-home functions, and the like.

Related Services: The "other things" that are so much a part of a wedding, including flowers, fashion, and photography.

Planning and Consulting: Details about organization, planning, and carrying out the consultant's role; and understanding the bride's emotions.

The Professional Bridal Consultant designation is good for three years, at which time it can be renewed or the wedding planner can move up to the next level.

Accredited Bridal Consultant

At this level consultants must be an association member for three years, as well as a Professional Bridal Consultant for the same amount of time. Candidates must complete a proficiency exam and participate in any association workshop, seminar, or annual conference. Candidates must also supply recommendations from three colleagues and three clients. In addition, candidates must respond to an essay question and pay a processing fee.

Master Bridal Consultant

After three years as an Accredited Bridal Consultant, consultants can again renew that designation or progress to Master Bridal Consultant. Requirements include a total of at least six years of membership in the Association of Bridal Consultants with three years as an Accredited Bridal Consultant. In addition to a proficiency exam, participation in additional seminars or conferences, and recommendations from peers and clients, candidates must also pay a processing fee and, during an annual conference, present a portfolio of a recent wedding. A portfolio will also help planners secure future clients. In your portfolio include references or testimonials from previous satisfied clients, copies of the invitation, newspaper announcements, photographs of the decorations and table settings, and any other pertinent visual details that will sell your abilities.

Participants must also complete one of the following:

- write and have published a wedding-related story or book
- present a wedding-related educational program
- participate in an electronic media talk show or feature program
- serve as an association state coordinator for at least one year
- serve as an officer for another major wedding-related association

Applications for membership and course work can be found online at bridalassn.com.

The Association of Bridal Consultants also offers a course called "Wedding as a Business." This course assists new consultants in writing a business plan. Topics include everything from setting fees to working with the first bride. Upon completion of the course, candidates can have their new business plans officially evaluated for an extra fee.

To read a testimonial about the Association of Bridal Consultants' Professional Development Program, go to bridalassn.com and click on "Professional Education." You can find course fees at the website as well.

Weddings Beautiful Worldwide

Weddings Beautiful Worldwide, a division of the National Bridal Service (NBS), offers self-study courses that allow students to proceed at their own pace. Most take six to twelve months for completion.

Both established wedding coordinators and those who are interested in starting their own business coordinating weddings could benefit from the training. In addition, Weddings Beautiful Worldwide courses cater to those in wedding-related businesses such as florists, photographers, caterers, gift registries, jewelers, bridal shops owners, and others.

The training course has eighteen assignments designed to educate students on a career as a wedding coordinator, whether self-employed or working for another enterprise. Each assignment is graded with notes and/or corrections. Upon completion students are awarded a Certified Wedding Specialist certificate.

Doris Nixon, president of Weddings Beautiful Worldwide, says, "Long ago Socrates wrote, 'Only through the humble acknowledgment of ignorance can wisdom be born.' Wise is the person who seeks to be educated before starting a business to plan weddings." With students in more than forty countries and available in two languages, the Weddings Beautiful Worldwide Home Study Course is a detailed road map for those seeking to establish a successful wedding planning business. Etiquette, traditions, motivation, and detailed how-to information are included in the course. "Certified Wedding Specialist is more than a title or a certificate. It's a promise to brides that the person who displays the certificate is a professionally trained consultant, with an established code of ethics," says Doris.

Courses

Course topics, as stated in the association's online catalog, cover the following:

Time: This assignment is geared toward developing a consciousness of time.

Developing Your Business Plan: This assignment offers advice on getting started and information on how to price and market your services.

Your Business Forms and Contracts: This course gives exposure to forms for clients and vendors, including sample contracts and brochures.

Wedding Invitations: This is a course on protocol, with an opportunity to sell wedding invitations.

Developing Wedding Expertise: You will learn about bridal vendors and weddings in general.

Directing Protestant and Military Weddings: Included here are charts and timetables for the wedding rehearsal and day of the wedding, plus instructions for all attendants.

Directing Catholic and Jewish Weddings: Tells you what you need to know to direct a wedding of these faiths.

Directing African American, Hispanic, and Orthodox Weddings: Wedding coordinators need to know what to suggest for all types of weddings.

Receptions: This course covers locations, catering, flowers, decorating, and more.

All About Ethnic Traditions and the History of Wedding Traditions: This course provides essential background information.

Wedding Fashions: Here's a comprehensive overview of the five basic principles of fashion, including illustrations and a glossary of bridal gown and tuxedo details.

Tabletop Settings: You will get instruction on the three elements of table settings—dinnerware, stemware, and flatware—plus terms and illustrations for setting a table correctly.

Talk Less, Say More: You'll learn the art of good communication.

Developing Management Techniques and Skills: This course covers six basic techniques for acquiring managerial skills in business.

The Ultimate You—Personal Public Relations: This section helps students take an inward look and assess personal strengths and weaknesses as they learn more about what makes people tick.

Final Exam

After the eighteen assignments have been completed with satisfactory grades, students receive the title "Certified Wedding Specialist" and are given a certificate that can be framed and displayed in their office.

For more information on training with Weddings Beautiful Worldwide, visit its website at weddingsbeautiful.com.

3

INDEPENDENT EVENT PLANNERS

INDEPENDENT, OR SELF-EMPLOYED, event planners plan the same types of events that planners employed by professional organizations do. They organize conferences and meetings, weddings, parties, book signings, and more. Some are generalists, working on any type of event; others specialize in one particular area, such as writers' conferences or weddings.

They plan events for social purposes, for the purpose of publicity—for example, promoting a product or person—for education, for business gatherings, and for the personal or financial development of those who attend the event.

Independent planners generally start out solo, often organizing their first events from the comfort of a home office or even a kitchen table. Some have already worked in event planning for a production firm, corporation, or hotel and have decided to strike out on their own. Others are in a separate business altogether and organize their first events to promote that business. Still others start out with event planning as a specific career goal.

Making event planning a successful self-employment venture requires the following qualities:

- good organizational skills
- a detail-oriented personality
- perseverance
- good social skills
- contacts, or the ability to make contacts

Says Phyllis Cambria, co-owner of PartyPlansPlus.com and coauthor with her partner, Patty Sachs, of *The Complete Idiot's Guide to Throwing a Great Party*, "When starting a business, carefully research your market and create a total business plan. Remember, it's not that people plan to fail, they simply fail to plan."

Getting Started—Getting Contracts

Getting contracts, in part, requires making contacts. And making contacts, in part, depends on your experience with the type of event you want to plan. A writer, for example, who is a member of a writers' association, with some good networking and planning might be able to land a contract for the group's annual conference.

Stephanie Dooley, Director of Events for Enchantment Events, a division of Author's Venue, based in Albuquerque, New Mexico, started out as a writer who did just that. "I had never considered an event planning profession until after I became a writer. Writers' conferences are a huge component to the overall publishing industry. Writing is a solitary profession, so the meetings, conferences, seminars, and retreats have played a large part in information exchange, connections, networking, and learning.

"Before I founded Enchantment Events, I worked with the writers' organization SouthWest Writers in Albuquerque in their outreach program. I organized workshops and other programs for a year. When the opportunity arose to become the director for the 1999 SouthWest Writers' Conference, I took it. I found an untapped talent within myself for organization and overall meeting conception. I was good at it! And I enjoyed being able to merge my love for writing with the detail-intensive meeting planning."

When the time came to assign the task of organizing the next year's conference, Stephanie produced a proposal the group was happy with. "In proposals we present to prospective clients, I cover everything from how the sessions will be laid out, who will be invited to speak, how many banquets there will be, and what the budget will be."

It was after planning a couple of successful conferences for Southwest that Stephanie founded Enchantment Events. However, she soon found other agencies coming to her to plan their events. "Some were arts or writing related, but I had clients from government agencies, private companies, and others.

"After two years with Enchantment Events, I began negotiations with my current business partner to create a new company of writers' services, bringing Enchantment Events in as the event planning component.

"My partner and I decided there were gaps in the opportunities given to authors in the publishing industry. In other words, there was a step missing between learning how to write and becoming a successful author. Networking is a major part of a published author's continued success. Although we didn't want to forgo the learning process altogether, our emphasis is on providing opportunities for experienced writers to push their careers into high gear.

"I still do what I did before, but I have the opportunity to be a part of the publishing industry in a direct way. The events my company produces internally are designed to help writers get published, and I have complete control over the quality of those events. It's extremely gratifying to see the result in helping other writers."

Most independent event planners rely on word of mouth. A satisfied customer comes back for more and spreads the good news. Some planners use the Yellow Pages, and most these days have professional websites to attract new business. An Internet search will reveal many professional website designers advertising their services.

Some self-employed planners hook up with related businesses. For example, an independent wedding planner will make herself or himself known to bridal shops and florists, to photographers and caterers. Often a bride will contact a caterer first, for example, then not know what to do next. Referrals often come in that way. And it works both ways. The savvy event planner keeps a record of all those vendors who refer clients, so when it comes time that a client needs a bridal gown, flowers, a photographer, or a caterer, the planner can send business back the way it came. This is a mutual relationship that works well for all parties.

Belonging to the Chamber of Commerce could bring in leads, and it certainly would create goodwill for yourself in the community. Visiting businesses and professionals you'd like to organize events for and leaving a business card and color brochure could also eventually pay off. To sell yourself and your business you need to get yourself and your name out there and build up some credits and a portfolio. Have something impressive to show a prospective client. A good track record speaks for itself.

Planning the Event

Planning an event involves many steps. "I work with two very different industries—the hospitality industry and the publishing industry," explains Stephanie. "So on one hand my day is spent contacting and negotiating with hotels for upcoming events. On the other, I spend time talking with authors, editors, and literary agents. I suspect many event planners find their expertise divided. Knowledge about the industry you plan conferences for is as important as knowing the event planning process. As both industries constantly fluctuate [hospitality and publishing in my case], I have to be on top of new trends."

One of the first tasks is defining the scope of the event and deciding what the purpose and final outcome should be. "I like the concept stage," says Stephanie Dooley. "I do constant research to see what's out there, what other meeting planners are doing. If there's anything I can incorporate into my own meetings to make them run more smoothly, to give the attendees more than they bargained for, I'll try it at least once. Dreaming up what your final product will look like, feel like, what the attendees will come away with, is exciting and fun. I like the travel and dealing with the decision makers. It makes me feel like I'm making a lasting contribution by going straight to the top (whether at a hotel or a publishing house) and swapping ideas and experience.

"Once we have determined why a group is having an event," says Stephanie, "we set the budget. A budget is the single most important item an event will have. More important than the speakers, the workshops, or the special events or excursions." The budget covers vitals such as the rent for the venue, decorations, speakers, catering, and so on. A big budget might allow for the most expensive hotel, or a laser show, or catering by a top restaurant. A smaller budget might lend itself to a garden party with hot dogs and hamburgers on the grill. What the client can afford will determine how far the planner can go.

"Once the budget is settled," Stephanie Dooley continues, "then the fun begins. We have to find a venue and agree upon terms."

Hotels work with contracts, specifying all the details, such as how many rooms the planner is booking—both conference rooms and sleeping rooms for out-of-town attendees and speakers—and what the rates are. Stephanie says, "Working with the venue is another task altogether. The hospitality industry is a whole new world, with its own language, set of rules, and duties. Extensive knowledge of hotel contracts is a must."

Contracts will specify what kind of refund to expect if the rooms aren't booked—and what kind of bonus to expect if your registrations exceed expectations. The contract will cover food costs and breaks and any audiovisual equipment that you order. In other words, everything you need from that venue should be put in writing to protect yourself and the event.

"Once a good contract is determined," says Stephanie Dooley, "most of the hotel contact is just maintenance. But one wrinkle can send the whole deal into a big mess. A date off, unanticipated attrition (a hotel term that basically means penalties) can all mean a struggle.

"We set a schedule, taking into account everything from how long attendees can sit through a single workshop to bathroom breaks, how much time it takes to go from class to class, to how many workshops can be squeezed into any given time. It's not enough to get it all down on paper and have catchy titles for the classes. We must be able to walk through the event to make sure it makes sense.

"Then we begin to add the faculty. Of course, we think about who might be right even as we decide on the scope of the event, but it is at this point we begin the phone calls and speakers' contracts. Again, this can be a lengthy process. Speakers who would be perfect for an event might have schedule conflicts, or their fee requirements might not fit the budget. A $10,000 to $50,000 fee for a name author such as Stephen King would be outside the budget for most writers' conferences. Local writers might volunteer to speak for free or for a small honorarium of $50 to $100.

"Signing speakers for a writers' conference is an ongoing process. Editors or agents could unexpectedly cancel as late as the day before the event."

Organization and Record Keeping

The amount of time required to pull an event off is not something you can glance over once a week and expect to be successful, warns Stephanie. "This is something some corporation executives unfortunately don't understand. They believe they can either do it themselves or pawn it off onto secretaries. Event planning—no matter how 'small' the event—is incredibly time-consuming.

"While planning the actual event isn't a drag, it can become overwhelming. When I look at the calendar and realize I have four or five events coming up in the next three months, and I've had two or three cancellations, and my events manager is on vacation, well, it can become quite tiresome. There are so many details to keep on top of, and when there are multiple conferences to maintain, it's like throwing fifteen or twenty lead balls in the air and making sure they all stay up. Organizational skills are a must. You must like details and be good at multitasking. An event planner juggles many things, and if you don't keep it straight, you'll have a lot of very frustrated people on your hands.

"Joining a local meeting planner's group is a good place to get basic information. There are degrees in the hospitality industry available, but most independent planners rely on more grassroots training, turning to organizational workshops and certification."

Keeping good records is also something every event planner has to do. Stephanie Dooley explains. "I have a home office with roughly five large file cabinets—not to mention shelves and a closet full of supplies. Basically my office is overflowing with things I need everyday to make the business run. I keep a file on each state in the United States and some foreign countries with hotel portfolios. That way, if I have an event in a particular city, I have a place to start."

Also, keeping track of speakers is important. Stephanie Dooley keeps files on possible speakers and speakers' bureaus. "A single conference that I organize can hold anywhere from ten to sixty faculty members. Although some of the tasks can be turned over to the contracted travel agent, members of the faculty must be kept informed of conference developments as well as the biographies, photos, session descriptions, and other materials they must provide us with. All of this takes an enormous amount of time."

Marketing

Marketing the event is a major component of making an event successful. Unless it's a corporate event or meeting with all of the employees attending, someone is responsible for seeing that the attendance fees will cover the budget.

"Marketing is ongoing and can take a lot of planning," says Stephanie Dooley. "We place ads, send out press releases, and make up flyers. Because Author's Venue does its own events, our planning team and marketing committee must assess where the best places to advertise might be.

The Event Itself

Once the big day arrives, the onsite coordination phase begins. This is where anything can happen. It is the coordinator's responsibility to keep the hotel in which the event will be held on its toes, keep everything happening on time, and smooth over disgruntled attendees, or even speakers.

"It usually means I work a fifteen-hour day with a clipboard attached to my hip," says Stephanie. "However, here is where I believe I excel. On-the-spot problem solving can be very satisfying. Customer satisfaction is the most important thing to an independent event planner, and when I can make everyone at least satisfied, if not happy, it's worth every blister and paper cut. All in all, it's the details that are the biggest part of my job—making sure nothing falls through the cracks."

Earnings

Salary structure is all over the place in this industry. A new planner working at a mid-sized hotel can probably expect to earn around $20,000 to $30,000 a year. An independent planner will get paid per event. Because of the work involved, most independent planners should expect between $10,000 and $20,000 per event. This would be for larger conferences, with a large faculty and multiple sub-events.

A basic standard would be to estimate a proposal based on $50 to $100 per hour, depending on your experience and years in the industry. But that depends on the location. A Chicago or New York City market would bear a higher hourly wage than, say, Albuquerque or Little Rock.

Stephanie Dooley says, "As a business owner, I rely solely on the success of the event, taking a share of the profit. This makes the success particularly important because if it flops, I don't get paid."

Expenses

Self-employed planners have expenses that planners employed by companies do not. Initially, they must pay for training and certification. Then, if not working from a home office, independent event planners have rent, phone, and utility bills to pay. They also have to purchase office furniture and supplies.

In addition, event planners need a nice wardrobe and a comfortable car to drive clients to potential venues or to meet with possible vendors. They have advertising expenses, and they also have to pay for insurance, which will include health plans for themselves and employees. They must also carry liability insurance to protect clients and themselves and their business against any mishaps. There's a lot to think about and plan for. Is the event safe? Does your table or booth layout meet fire codes? Are your linens, drapery, and candles approved by the fire department? Have you made the event handicapped accessible? Does the caterer you hired meet health code requirements? Do you have enough liability insurance?

You also have to think about workman's compensation and if you have permission to record and/or play licensed music. Are you following all union regulations? Will the electricity carry the load of the equipment brought in? It's not enough to rely on the insurance a particular venue might carry.

All of this adds up to money, and the new planner will need some savings to rely on. Those who don't have appreciable savings can start small, working from a home office, and build up a reputation and a clientele before making a commitment to office space.

Training and Certification

Although many self-employed planners fly by the seat of their pants, so to speak, stacking up on-the-job training, more and more people these days seek professional training through the few university programs available and certification through the field's professional associations. For those not wanting long training programs, the professional associations offer some short-term courses that can even be participated in through online classes and E-mail. Chapter 2 covers in depth the training any event planner can benefit from, as well as the certification related professional associations offer.

Sample Job Listings

Here are some sample want ads for jobs to give you an idea of the types of positions available. Your own search will reveal similar job listings.

Job Title: Meeting Planner

Type of Organization: Special event design and production company

Location: New Mexico

Position Description: A special event design and production company is currently looking for a self-motivated individual who is intrigued by the idea of working with an intensely creative team, confident enough in his/her abilities to work on a commission-only basis, and attracted by the prospect of flexible hours with essentially unlimited income potential. Our primary focus is to design, produce, and plan special events for corporate customers. In addition, our full-service and on-site production shop allows us to assist customers in areas such production/decorating and set design. We also have the expertise to offer meeting logistics coordination, on-site meeting management, destination management, and other meeting and event-related services. It is the goal of this position to expand our current base business and actively seek new corporate customers.

This position will actively manage the sales process by:

- prospecting for new corporate customers
- creating new customers with direct sales techniques
- maintaining and cultivating customer relationships
- building a process for repeat business
- working with our creative team to develop effective and convincing proposals
- meeting and (ideally) exceeding sales volume goals

Qualifications and Experience: Two years minimum of experience in direct sales is required. Proficiency in office computer systems is required. You must have a background in either hotel sales and/or event industry sales management. Existing customer relationships and a strong client base is required.

Salary: Compensation is 100 percent commission with $40,000 to $55,000 projected based on first year goals; however, potential is unlimited.

Contact Information: Please submit résumé and cover letter via E-mail.

Job Title: Convention Project Manager

Type of Organization: Meetings and event management company

Location: Missouri

Position Description: Seeking convention manager(s) full-time to lead convention and event projects with integrated team of experts.

Qualifications and Experience: Must have relevant experience in meetings management with proven track record and ability to demonstrate systems for planning. At least five or more years of experience preferred. Must have full computer abilities, creativity, team focus, ability to travel up to fifteen weeks annually, ability to take initiative, and excellent client references.

Salary: $40,000 negotiable and opportunity for commissions for bringing new projects to the firm. Long-term equity potential as well.

Contact Information: Send résumé by fax or E-mail attachment.

4

WEDDING PLANNERS

HAVE YOU EVER attended a large wedding or read about one in a
magazine and wondered what went on behind the scenes to create
such a well-coordinated affair? Although definitely considered
events, weddings are in a class by themselves and merit special
attention. They require the same eye-for-detail qualities that any
event does, but with weddings there's something more. To be successful in this sector, wedding planners must be romantics at heart.

Any wedding planner will tell you how helping a couple's special day come off without any problems provides real satisfaction.
The tears in the mother of the bride's eyes, the hug the groom
gives the wedding planner when she or he helps pin on his bou-
tonniere, and the bride, full of thanks for all the planner's support
and encouragement—all of this contributes to the wedding planner's sense of fulfillment for a job well done. Just knowing that you
were instrumental in participating in the most important day of a

couple's life can compensate for all the hard work. And romance aside, it is hard work and strict attention to detail that go into organizing a wedding.

Wedding Details

Any bride who's organized her own wedding knows what's involved in pulling off a topnotch event. Just look at some of the details:

- setting a date
- obtaining the necessary licenses
- arranging financing
- reserving the location for the wedding ceremony
- reserving the location for the reception
- engaging the services of the person to perform the ceremony
- choosing a menu
- choosing or arranging for china and silverware
- ordering tables, cloths, tents, etc., if an outdoor event
- ordering flowers and coordinating their delivery
- designing and printing napkins or matchbooks
- hiring musicians
- hiring a photographer
- choosing bridesmaids, ushers, the best man, the flower girl, the ring bearer
- ordering the cake and its centerpiece
- creating an invitation list
- designing and ordering invitations
- addressing, stamping, and mailing invitations
- arranging for transportation and/or accommodation for out-of-town guests

- arranging for transportation to the wedding ceremony and reception

There's more—don't forget the wedding dress, bridesmaids' gowns, and clothing for the mother of the bride, the flower girl, and the groom. There are wedding accessories, too, such as the wedding album and the toast glasses. After all that, there's the honeymoon and the planning that it involves.

Although some brides organize these events with the help of mothers, sisters, and friends, others look for professional expertise. And that's where you'd come in.

What Wedding Planners Do

First and foremost, wedding planners take the pressure off the bride and her family. They handle most of the details mentioned above, either doing the work themselves or contracting it out to other vendors. Established wedding planners have a list of contacts for most of the following services:

- catering (including tables, chairs, china, as well as food)
- bakeries and cake decorators
- bridal shops
- printing
- florists
- hotel ballrooms or other facilities
- musicians
- photographers and videographers

Planners need to know how to communicate with all different types of vendors. It's important that the wedding planner (or any other type of event planner) have a working knowledge of catering, photography, lighting, tents, floral arrangements, contracts, and so on. It's a good idea also to be aware of all the latest innovations in these industries.

Says planner and author Phyllis Cambria, "This is an area where many so-called planners fail. They think only about their portion of the event. More to the point, what they perceive is their portion of the event."

The first step is to meet with the bride and her family. There is much to discuss: the bride's vision for her wedding, as well as her mother's vision, and the family's budget. It may be that not all family members agree. Often it's the job of the wedding planner to act as mediator, calming heated emotions and finding workable compromises.

A professional wedding planner can save the bride time and money. The planner is trained in all of the etiquette and procedures involved with coordinating wedding ceremonies and receptions.

A wedding planner will be able to answer all the bride's questions. She or he is trained in dealing with special circumstances, too. What do you do if the bride's parents are divorced? What is the role of each family member? Who pays for what? Whose names appear on the invitation? Who dances with whom and in what order?

The wedding planner also knows how to set tables properly and is familiar with the differences in china, porcelain, and pottery.

A wedding planner knows all the rules—and also when they can be broken. The planner's expertise saves the bride and her family from all the worry that can usually accompany this special but stressful event.

Trained wedding planners know how to give advice, and they also know not to impose their own ideas. They can listen, plan, organize, and befriend. Because they are objective third parties, they can be diplomatic when disagreements arise.

Once the type of wedding is established, including the budget, the wedding planner calculates the fee, and then gets to work. Most planners try to get as much a head start as possible—maybe eight months to a year in advance of the event. They have a schedule they follow: what to do six months in advance, what to do three months in advance, one month, one week, and one day in advance. Sometimes, though, the best schedules go by the wayside. A client might be planning a wedding only a month away or the hotel or the caterer or the florist went out of business and now it's the planner's job to scramble to find a new one.

An ability to pay close attention to detail is the most important quality a wedding planner can possess. After that comes the ability to remain calm under pressure. A good sense about human relations and good communication skills are next in line.

A wedding planner keeps busy, juggling all aspects of an event. A successful planner will have more than one event to juggle. At that point many new planners start expanding their business, hiring help, either full- or part-time.

The rewards can be many, but the work can take its toll. Most weddings take place on the weekend. And in the spring, the busiest time for weddings, a planner could have back-to-back events without a moment to breathe.

This is not a career for a person wanting to work a nine-to-five, Monday-through-Friday job. While other events, such as for a corporate client, might take place during the week, social events usually fill up a planner's time day and night.

"Realize this is a business," says Gerard J. Monaghan, president of the Association of Bridal Consultants. "A fun business to be sure, but a business nonetheless. You need to be professional. Join the appropriate professional organizations. Develop your business plan and marketing plan, and establish your base of vendors before you even think of working with brides.

"Learn as much as you can about the wedding business in general, and consulting in general. Network with other wedding professionals. Develop your own specialties. There are about two and a half million weddings a year in the United States; there is no need to be ultra competitive. You can't handle all of them.

"Bridal/wedding consulting is a relatively inexpensive business to establish, but doing it right is time and labor intensive."

Where Wedding Planners Work

Although many event and meeting coordinators offer full-service planning, some planners specialize only in weddings. The vast majority of wedding planners are self-employed. They set up shop from home or rent office space. Others work for hotels (see Chapter 5 for information on hotel event planning) or through bridal shops. With the latter, the wedding planner could own the shop and provide a wedding consultation service along with bridal gowns and other accessories. Or the bridal shop owner could refer clients to a trusted planner, perhaps for a small commission.

Location, Location, Location

If you decide to open your own bridal shop, consider your location carefully. Businesses just starting out need high visibility to benefit from walk-in customers. But new businesses might lack the funds to pay the high rents most malls charge. If that's the case, then research other locations. Would your shop be visible from a major highway? Could you find available space in a downtown area that receives a lot of foot traffic?

If you're thinking positively, you might decide to pay the higher rent for better visibility with the hopes that your shop will eventually pay off. In a year or two, that high rent won't seem so bad if your income is appreciable. As a rule of thumb, make sure to have enough back-up money when starting an enterprise to cover your rent for a year.

A Seasonal Business

In part, your success as a wedding planner will depend on the season. In the Northeast and other areas with long winters, bridal season starts in April and continues strong through the end of June. It picks up again in September and runs through the second week of November. In the far South where cold weather is rare, the season can run through the winter. During the high season, wedding planners can be extremely busy, sometimes with several weddings in one weekend.

Professional Associations for Wedding Planners

Two wedding-related professional associations exist to help planners get trained and established. Here's an up-close look at them. (Turn to Appendix A for full address information.)

Association of Bridal Consultants

Based in New Milford, Connecticut, the Association of Bridal Consultants was founded in 1981. It has about twenty-five hundred members in twenty-eight countries. The Association of Bridal

Consultants is a membership service organization, designed to increase awareness of the wedding business and improve the professionalism of members.

Those who join receive a newsletter, insurance for their business, consultation with experts when questions or problems arise, help designing business brochures, and an educational program with professional certification. Members also receive discounts on books and magazines and help with job placement and advertising. The association maintains a referral system to help members get new clients.

The association's professional development program, available through distance-learning, offers three trademarked professional designations: Professional Bridal Consultant, Accredited Bridal Consultant, and Master Bridal Consultant. (For more information on the association's training program, turn to Chapter 2.)

Weddings Beautiful Worldwide/National Bridal Service

Weddings Beautiful Worldwide is a division of the National Bridal Service, an organization for independent wedding consultants. National Bridal Service (NBS) has been in business since 1951. NBS is a membership organization with more than twelve hundred independently owned businesses that serve the bridal market. Its mission is "to provide a continuous flow of ideas, methods, policies and recommendations which will give our members a competitive advantage within their local markets and result in each member enjoying greater sales, greater operating efficiency, and greater cash profits."

Its benefits and services are similar to those of a national franchise. However, there is a major difference. Unlike with franchises, NBS members maintain complete control of their business and all decision making.

The National Bridal Service has several divisions. Weddings Beautiful Worldwide is the planning, coordinating, and directing division of NBS. The NBS Weddings Beautiful Worldwide Division is a specialized home-study training program and continuous educational service for professional wedding planners and coordinators. (See Chapter 2 for more information about the Weddings Beautiful Worldwide training program.) The program is used by those who own or are considering starting their own business coordinating weddings or to complement another wedding-related business such as florist, photographer, caterer, gift registry, bridal shop, and so forth.

Members of this organization receive benefits similar to those offered by the Association of Bridal Consultants, including a newsletter, consultations, advertising help, a logo to put on pamphlets and letterhead, and recommended suppliers for invitations, accessories, and attendant gifts.

Other divisions of the NBS include:

- Fashion Division
- Jewelry Division
- Gift Division
- Tuxedo Division
- Custom Catalog Service Division
- Custom Internet Service Division
- The Bridal Council of America Division

Training for Wedding Planners

Event planners come to the profession from all sorts of backgrounds with a variety of training. Some are self-taught; some learn on the job; some earn a degree in event planning, public relations, hospitality, or a related area; some event planners have taken event-planning courses.

The two professional associations mentioned above offer training programs that award specific designations wedding planners could use to advertise their services. The programs teach students through correspondence-type courses, and future wedding planners can study at their own pace. Subjects include everything from how to make a business plan to how to plan an ethnic wedding.

How Wedding Planners Are Paid

Wedding planners who work for hotels or other establishments can be paid an annual salary or part salary/part commission. The amount would vary, depending upon the size of the employer's budget and the price tag it puts on wedding planning services. The higher-end the service it provides and the more money it takes in, and the more the wedding planner would be compensated.

Self-employed wedding planners also have a choice how to be paid. Some estimate the number of hours they'll need to complete the job and charge an hourly rate. With experience, wedding planners can learn to be accurate estimators. Over time, instead of an hourly rate, they might choose to calculate a flat fee based on the amount of time they'll need to put in to do the job.

Other wedding planners charge a percentage of the client's overall wedding budget. For example, if a client plans a $10,000 wedding, the consultant could charge 10 to 15 percent and earn between $1,000 and $1,500. With several weddings going at once, this can add up nicely.

Wedding planning, in general, is a seasonal business. Most weddings occur either in the spring or the fall—with a big dip in business over the summer—and through the winter months. As a result, some wedding planners prefer to make a set annual salary working for someone else—or they choose to operate a related business such as jewelry sales or running a bridal shop.

A Bridal Shop Owner

No day is more important to a bride than her wedding day. And no one knows that better than Donna Lemire, owner of Illusions, a full-service bridal shop in Tyngsboro, Massachusetts.

Donna Lemire opened her shop in 1994 and since then has been providing wedding apparel, accessories, and consultation and wedding coordination for countless brides and their families.

She has worked in the field approximately twenty-four years, starting with wedding cakes and floral arrangements, then moving into wedding consulting.

To train herself she has taken a variety of courses over the years, including cake decorating, floral design, and a wedding specialist course through Weddings Beautiful Worldwide.

That First Year

"Due to a personal tragedy in 1991 (I lost my son in an automobile accident) I needed to change careers. I was unhappy with my current life and wanted to work with happy people. I brought my cake business and florals, including some giftware, into the business first. Nice thought, but the people coming in were brides who needed more—for example, dresses.

"I knew it was time to either invest in inventory, or give it up. My overhead was high and I was virtually unknown. Even though my cakes and flowers were beautiful, they didn't pay the bills.

"I started by contacting bridal manufacturers and buying some dresses. Before I knew it, I had a fully stocked bridal shop. My first season I had 24 dresses. I now have 140 bridal gowns, about 200 bridesmaids gowns, flower girl dresses, dresses for the mother of the bride, more than 150 headpieces, shoes, jewelry, and a full line of wedding accessories, such as unity candles, toast glasses, bridal garters, bridal gift sets, cake knives, and guest books. I also make silk floral arrangements and wedding cakes and have a range of rental items, including tuxedos, floral trees and arrangements, and card holders for the reception. In addition, I consult and sell wedding invitations, and as a coordinator, I have the contacts to arrange a full wedding, regardless of the budget.

"My first year was difficult because I was virtually unknown. I took out ads in the bridal section of all the local newspapers. I also advertised in bridal magazines—which worked the best. It is also important to advertise in the Yellow Pages of the telephone book, and an 800-number lends credibility. I placed ads in church bulletins and made up place mats, which didn't work. In addition, I did a few bridal fashion shows. Overall, the most important thing is to get your name out there. I also joined the Better Business Bureau, but I felt that was a waste of money. You don't need to be a member, just do a good job. If there are no complaints against you, no one can hurt you.

"Most of my new business that first year came from referrals. I received numerous thank you notes and pictures of previous brides and grooms I had helped."

Wedding Coordinator

"Being a coordinator enables me to take my services one step further. A couple can walk into my shop with no direction, and walk out having everything they need with a minimum of legwork. Even if they do not require a coordinator, I supply them with business cards for whatever they need. There is no charge for a referral. I tell them to meet with the people, ask for references, view their work, and do not commit to anything until they have met with a few vendors for each service required.

"If they hire me for the coordinating, I interview and hire the vendors. Being a full-service shop requires me to put more time into my clients. I am concerned with their wedding, not just what they choose to wear.

"The only people who survive this business are the ones who genuinely love it. Being around so much happiness has brought me closer to my own husband. Most of the time, I would have to classify it as a labor of love. I spent two hours once with a bride who was not sure of her feelings. We talked until long after I closed the shop. Sometimes when family gets too involved in the festivities, these girls need someone to talk to who isn't Mom or Dad. They are looking for someone to tell them the prenuptial jitters are common. They are so afraid to tell their parents they have doubts because of the money being spent, that they keep it all inside until some of them are so miserable they don't enjoy the time before their wedding. How many times have we heard a bride say, 'I'll be glad when this is over.'

"By having a wedding coordinator to listen and talk with, my brides are not so likely to get overwhelmed with the mounting questions they are afraid to ask a relative. Along with the festivities goes anxiety, fear, and being able to accept change gracefully. It is hard enough as human beings to cope with one of those feelings at a time, let alone all of them at once. It is enough for any bride to ask herself if she is doing the right thing. When I am asked about any of these things, my first question is always, 'Do you love him?' If the answer is yes, then I proceed with the stories of the many other brides with whom I have had the same conversation.

"It is a service-oriented business, and the commitment is enormous, if you are doing your job the way you should be."

The Upsides and the Downsides

"The part of my job I love the most is pleasing a bride—which is not an easy accomplishment. It takes a lot of patience and hand holding, but when you feel appreciated, you don't mind so much.

"A lot of these girls are very sweet until a few weeks before their wedding. Then they all turn into lunatics because they are so stressed out."

Charging for Your Services

"Most consultants charge for their services in two ways: some get a percentage of the entire wedding. Initially the charge on a percentage basis is 10 percent. As you become more successful, you may charge 15 percent. Others charge an hourly rate, anywhere from $25 to $50 per hour; it depends on how little or how much you do. Most of the coordinating I do is based on an hourly basis. I believe that is fairest to the bride. I have other income from my shop—

dresses, tuxedo rentals, and other accessories. If I were working from my home, as some coordinators do, obviously I would be a little more flexible with my fee schedule. I have a business within a business, so I am obligated to other duties within my shop.

"If I ever sell the shop, and decide to do only wedding coordinating, I will probably charge a percentage of the wedding. I believe it is the most lucrative because most weddings exceed $10,000. At 10 percent, a coordinator can expect a salary of $1,000.

"With the income from selling dresses and other things, I usually make about that per wedding, after expenses. I guess it all works out. The shop is a double-edged sword, the expenses are high, but the brides come to me. I am sure I could book any number I want, but I prefer to screen them first before I decide if I want to coordinate their wedding."

A Full-Service Event Planning Company

Mary Tribble is the president and owner of Tribble Creative Group, an event planning and production company located in Charlotte, North Carolina. Tribble Creative Group handles social events such as weddings, anniversaries, and bar mitzvahs; corporate events; hospitality programs, welcoming receptions, and awards ceremonies; and tours and transportation.

Tribble Creative Group also offers consulting to both entrepreneurial and institutional establishments that support the hospitality industry. It provides team-building sessions, creativity training workshops, customized customer service training, leadership development, and strategic marketing plans.

Mary Tribble earned her B.A. in art history in 1982 from Wake Forest University in Winston-Salem, North Carolina. She was also one of the first to earn the Certified Special Events Professional (CSEP) designation from the International Special Events Society (ISES). She has attended countless continuing education courses through industry conventions. She is also frequently asked to speak on event planning at regional and national conventions.

Getting Started

"I was working at an advertising agency as an account executive, when one of my clients asked the agency to plan a grand opening event for its new offices. As a special project, it ended up being my responsibility. It was a huge event—a black tie gala with a laser light show—and I loved every minute of the planning. I knew I wanted to be involved in events from that time on. At first, we opened a small division at the agency for event planning, but I soon went out on my own. I was twenty-four at the time.

"I started with nothing more than a Rolodex, sitting on my bed in my apartment. No computer, nothing. I got a loan for $5,000 from a friendly investor, which helped me pay my bills until the checks started coming in. That was sixteen years ago.

"After about two years in business, I rented a small office, then hired my first employee. A few years later I hired two more employees. I now have twelve employees—which is a gracious plenty as far as I'm concerned.

"Now that the industry has gotten so much more sophisticated, I'm not sure I'd be able to get by the way I did back then. Clients want event planners who are educated in their industry and carry all the proper insurance—and all that takes money. I have very nice offices in downtown Charlotte, and I think that adds credibility to my company.

"Now, because I've been around so long, I get a lot of my business through word-of-mouth, but I still have to market my services. That's usually through phone calls and sending out my brochure to prospects.

"I don't do much advertising. I'm very active in the Chamber of Commerce and I'm a member of our Convention and Visitors Bureau and the International Special Events Society. A lot of business comes through networking with those groups. I now have a website, too: tribblecreativegroup.com.

"We're not a cookie-cutter social event consultant company. Tribble Creative Group has a select social clientele that demands quality and originality in design, because its guests have experienced the best. Our clients turn to us to deliver even more.

"At Tribble Creative Group, we don't just consult, we produce the event. We're there every step of the way, providing creative design, vendor management, logistics, etiquette recommendations, and entertainment management. Whether it's selecting a unique seating cardholder or directing technical cues at the reception, we provide full-service event production."

A Typical Day

"It's crazy, stress-filled, but fun. A good example of a typical day would be:

7:30 A.M. Meeting with a client about a huge event we're planning.

9:00 Back to the office to re-work a budget for a
wedding client. (The mother wanted it all, but the
father had called me into his office—without his
wife—to tell me what he was willing to spend.)
10:30 Meeting with a client about another event.
12:00 P.M. Off to exercise, then lunch at desk.
1:00 Sales calls during the first part of the afternoon.
2:30 Brainstorming meeting with staff. Interrupted by a
call from a client to put together an event in a week.
Reconvened staff to brainstorm again.
4:00 Worked on writing up a proposal.
5:30 Visited a potential site for a rehearsal dinner.
6:30 Time to go home.

"My days are rarely, if ever, relaxed. A typical day has three to
six meetings plus phone calls, deadlines for proposals, budgeting,
payroll concerns, dealing with employees' problems, making sales
calls, doing diagrams of event layouts, trudging around construc-
tion sites, meeting with vendors and clients, fielding phone calls
from people who want to pick my brain about the event business,
and so on.

"The work atmosphere is usually what I'd describe as 'frantic
fun.' I try to run a flexible company with a sense of humor—practical jokes are encouraged—but I expect everyone to roll up their
sleeves and get the job done.

"In the busy season, I work 60 to 65 hours a week. When it's
less busy, about 50. My employees work about 45 to 50 hours,
since they only work events they are assigned to (I'm usually at
them all)."

Wedding Bell Blues

"Weddings can be especially difficult to plan because there are so many personalities involved. With a corporate client, I'm usually answering to one person, and that person has usually reached a consensus with his or her staff as to what the event should be. With a wedding, the bride, the mother of the bride, the father of the bride, the in-laws, and the groom all have different expectations.

"The bride—and the mother of the bride—have been dreaming of this day for twenty-some years, so their expectations are very high. The father of the bride is usually worried about what the costs will be, and he can't understand why the bride's mother wants to spend $2,000 on placecard holders. There have been times when the mother of the bride, the bride, and the father of the bride are diametrically opposed, and I've had to step into some very tense situations, acting as mediator. It can be a very emotional experience for all concerned, and it's my job to stay calm and bring everyone to a consensus.

"It's also my job to exceed the twenty-some years of expectations—create a fairy-tale wedding that the bride will remember forever—whatever her style or taste. One month that might mean a casual lakeside wedding with a rustic wedding canopy covered with lavender, roses, and vines. The next it could be a glittering-gold wedding patterned after Versailles in a hotel ballroom, with huge gold candelabra centerpieces.

"That particular glittering-gold wedding was something I had only three and half weeks to plan—and it was for five hundred people! The groom's mother was ill, and the wedding had been reset for six months earlier. But all were concerned that she might not make it. So, bam! We had to plan a huge gala in less than a month—in a different hotel than had been originally reserved.

"For all the events I work with, we come up with the ideas, then plan the whole thing from start to finish—invitations, catering, decorating, special effects, entertainment, and more. We contract all that out, though. We don't keep lasers in stock!

"Paying attention to the details is the most important part of event planning. We can come up with all the wonderful themes in the world, but if we don't interpret them with details, they mean nothing. When we plan an event, everything—invitations, decorations, entertainment, place cards, gifts, signage—is selected to enhance the concept of the event.

"Also, the day-to-day planning is very detail oriented. We have to imagine an event from the time someone gets the invitation, to how they will get there, where they will park, who will greet them, how the event will begin, and how it will end.

"For every event, we create a schedule for setup, which is an hour-by-hour outline of everything that will happen leading up to the event. Sometimes, if it's a complicated event, that document can be ten to twelve pages long. We also create a show schedule that outlines the event itself.

"The rewards of wedding planning usually come when the bride walks into the reception for the first time and sees the effect we have created. If she gasps, I know we've done our job.

"What I like most about my work is the satisfaction that I've surpassed the client's dreams and expectations—that gasp factor. Also, I like the diversity—no day is ever the same, and I do get to spend a good deal of my time with creative people brainstorming new ideas and coming up with new challenges.

"I also get a rush from the stress the events create. I like to solve problems on my toes, and come up with quick and innovative solutions."

The Downside

"The long hours are a downside, though. It's not uncommon for us to work eighteen to twenty hours with no break—and I work a lot of weekends and evenings.

"Other downsides are dealing with all the details of the event—which is why I have employees. I like to conceptualize the event, but the drudgery of all the phone calls and meetings on minute things can be tiresome."

The Finances Involved

"Different planners charge different ways, and it's up to you to figure out what works best in your market. A way to do this would be, first of all, to join an association for event or wedding planning so you can network with others in your area. The Association of Bridal Consultants is strictly for wedding planners. The International Special Events Society covers the whole industry. (See Appendix A for addresses.)

"Having said that, some people charge an hourly fee, some charge a percentage of the overall budget, and others charge a combination of both. Usually, total fees will equal roughly 15 to 30 percent of the overall budget, using whichever method you choose.

"I personally always charge some kind of planning fee, even if I'm adding a percentage, because I think it's important for the client to perceive value in your services.

"In terms of potential annual earnings, that can vary widely from market to market, as you can imagine. I'd say for the first year or so not to count on earning much higher than in the $20,000s. You've got to develop a reputation first and then get business by recommendations from satisfied clients.

"Because most weddings are planned at least eight months out, it will be some time before those contracts come in. After three or four years of exemplary service to your clients, you could expect to earn $40,000 or so a year, depending on the city you serve. This could go much higher in large metropolitan areas, but a planner in a smaller market may never exceed that level.

"A word of warning when considering wedding planning as a career: Don't forget that weddings happen on weekends! You need to be prepared for a very heavy workload during the wedding season."

Advice from Mary Tribble

"Education, education, education! Just because you planned your sorority rush parties doesn't mean you can plan events professionally. We take on a great deal of responsibility when we put one thousand people in a hotel ballroom.

"Planning events is not all fun and games, and you must make sure you're providing your client with a safe and secure event. You need to stay atop of the cutting edge trends, and make sure your clients are getting the best services possible.

"The International Special Events Society has chapters all over the world, most of which offer monthly educational meetings. George Washington University now offers a degree in events management. *SpecialEvents Magazine* hosts an annual convention for more than three thousand event producers, with great education sessions. There are plenty of avenues now for you to get the education that even I didn't have when I started out.

"Even if you don't go for a specific event planning degree, degrees in public relations, marketing, or hotel/hospitality management can prepare you to some extent. Public relations courses very often include sections on events.

"In addition to education, you need hands-on experience. Volunteer on a committee for a local nonprofit organization's fundraiser. Intern at an event production company, hotel, or catering firm. The experience you receive will be a great investment.

"Make sure you have the perfect event planner personality. You need to be a left brain/right brain person. You need the creative side to come up with new and exciting ideas, but you also need the detail side to execute them. That's a tough combination.

"You also need to thrive on stress—and learn not to panic in bad situations. You need to be quick on your toes, you need to be a negotiator, and you need to have a calming influence on people. Our clients need someone calm and relaxed in the face of the controlled chaos."

A Party Planner Close-Up

Phyllis Cambria, along with Patty Sachs, owns and operates PartyPlansPlus.com, which has a website of the same name and is based in Coconut Creek, Florida. They are the authors of *The Complete Idiot's Guide to Throwing a Great Party* (Alpha Books/Macmillan, October 2000). They are also freelancers who write about parties and special events for various publications. They are professional speakers and celebration experts who work with clients to offer advice on weddings, parties, and other events. They also work on-site with their clients as needed.

Phyllis Cambria explains her business: "People can visit our website, where we have lots of free content, links to party supplies, and other resources that can help them plan their own parties. Or they can hire us to do a custom party plan for them. We have a phone, online, or E-mail consultation with our clients, and then we create a custom party plan for them.

"Patty Sachs, my partner, and I also do more traditional party and event planning coordination for local clients. Patty is in Jacksonville, Florida (about three hundred miles north of me) and occasionally does some party planning for clients up there. I do a bit more of it out of my location here in Coconut Creek. I'm more active in the hands-on projects than Patty is these days. She prefers the writing and general consultations. I like the challenge of both.

"I actually do every type of event: social, corporate, and nonprofit. When I was an in-house planner, I did thirty-five to forty-five events a year (many were fairly small events). Before the tragedy of 9/11, after which many, if not most, events were canceled or postponed, I would do about ten to fifteen events a year. They covered the spectrum: social events, bar/bat mitzvahs, corporate events (holiday parties, open houses, company picnics), wedding-related events (weddings, showers, bachelor/bachelorette parties), social events (birthdays, anniversaries, graduations, housewarmings), charity fund-raisers (galas, auctions, golf tournaments), and miscellaneous events.

"Since I suspect that the business decline is temporary as we work to make things go back to normal, those numbers are still pretty accurate.

"However, that does bring up another important point. For planners, how well our business does is greatly affected by the economy and world conditions. When we're at war as we are now or if the economy is down, our business is one of the first affected because people either don't feel like they want to entertain lavishly or because they can't afford to."

Getting Started

Phyllis Cambria has been planning parties and special events professionally for more than twenty years. "I began working for a special event company in 1988. Prior to that, I handled the special events and meetings as part of my job duties for several insurance companies." Phyllis also earned an associate's degree as a legal secretary.

"Much of my initial training was on the job. However, over the years, I have taken courses given through the International Special Events Society at The Special Event annual conferences sponsored by *SpecialEvents Magazine.*

"I also have a background in theater and film. This allows me to incorporate the training I received in lighting, set design, and staging into my special event experience.

"I have always loved planning parties and events. My parents were famous for their theme parties, and I enjoyed helping them plan those events. I worked on the committees for all the proms, dances, and homecoming celebrations, both in high school and college. Not surprisingly, that gave me some valuable experience.

"By the time I became engaged to be married, I understood all the aspects of planning that needed to be done to plan a successful wedding. From being in charge of so many other events and my training as a legal secretary, I understood contracts and how to find the best vendors for my own wedding.

"The research and planning book I put together to design my own wedding was so large, extensive, and detailed, I was able to use it later to help plan the weddings of many other friends.

"When I started working as an in-house event planner for a nonprofit, in my first ninety days, I was responsible for six major events. In fact, on the Thursday following my Monday start date, I was in charge of a large breakfast event of community leaders. I had to step in where the other planner had left off and make the event work. In fact, my predecessor had only done a minor amount of the work, and then my supervisor had stepped in (without much event experience) and continued the planning. Being experienced, I immediately recognized some potential problems and had to jump in and fix them before the event started. This was a true trial by fire, although it was not an uncommon one.

"Through an odd set of circumstances, I went to work for a friend who owned an entertainment agency. We were given the opportunity to plan numerous events and my training expanded.

"Shortly after that, the International Special Events Society was formed. This was an unequaled opportunity to network with other event professionals. We trained each other both informally and then formally when the organization began a series of educational programs on all aspects of events: decor, photography, videography, lighting, catering, sound, entertainment, transportation, security, operations, and other key elements to a successful event.

"I later went to work for Broward Community College, the second largest community college in Florida, as their special events coordinator. That gave me invaluable experience because I was responsible for producing forty to fifty events a year on a minimal budget.

"I have read almost every book on the subject and continue to supplement my education, while also training others in the profession.

"In 1999 Patty Sachs, whom I had met and corresponded with via the Internet, and I were given the opportunity to write *The Complete Idiot's Guide to Throwing a Great Party*, several freelance articles, and the website copy for some new party sites. We realized the Internet was a unique opportunity to extend our client base and we formed PartyPlansPlus.com."

The Day to Day

"There is no such thing as a typical day. Some days require that I spend the entire day working on a specific event. Other days I may juggle planning work on several events. Still others may mean that I am doing nothing more than seeking out and meeting new vendors, clients, prospects, and venues.

"I generally do some type of marketing each day. This might be directed at general marketing efforts, tracking down corporate clients who are coming to my area for an event, looking for new ways of finding clients, or keeping in touch with past clients.

"Some part of each day is generally devoted to education, too. Whether it's reading general trade publications or promotional materials of vendors, meeting with a supplier, researching a new product, ordering new product materials, or reading general business procedures or books that I believe will be helpful, I try to expand my knowledge each day.

"After the event, I generally hold a debriefing with my vendors and have a recap meeting with a client to make sure that everything was done to his or her satisfaction. With the vendors we determine what worked, what didn't, and how we might improve on future events.

"Remember, a coordinator has to know not only her job, but also the duties of anyone she hires. If she can't converse with a vendor in his or her language, then how can she know whether she is getting the proper service or a good price? For example, how can I order a *gobo* from my lighting vendor unless I know what one is, how it is used, what its capabilities or limitations are, and what it should cost to have it installed?"

Upsides and Downsides

"I actually enjoy the planning of the event more than the execution. It's lovely to see it all come together and see my client happy, but the act of creating and implementing an idea from scratch is the most fun for me. I also enjoy being able to come up with alternative plans when an original concept doesn't work or needs to be adjusted.

"Unfortunately, that is something I spend the least amount of time doing. The bulk of my time is spent marketing and finding new clients and/or projects.

"The downside of being an in-house planner is that you generally have a certain number of events that repeat each year with the same guest list. You get burned out easily trying to create something fresh and exciting with limited dollars to work with and a rigid set of goals that have to be accomplished.

"What often makes this process even more frustrating is that you design a great event and get the client all excited about it, but then the client turns around and reduces the budget drastically. He or she then wants you to accomplish the same task and give the type of party you originally proposed but using a lot less money. When that happens, you need to come up with creative alternatives to make the smaller budget stretch farther. It can't always be done, but you will often be asked to perform a miracle."

Salaries

"Salaries vary quite a bit, too, depending on location, experience, and type of business. An in-house planner can make anywhere from the upper teens to the low $40,000s. Some make more, but their duties generally extend past just creating events. They are also responsible for all other aspects of public relations and/or marketing.

"When you work for yourself, your salary capabilities are limited only by your ability to find clients and projects. There are planners who make less than $10,000 a year and some who make more than $1 million, but these planners are rare.

"A motivated and successful independent planner or one who works on commission for an event company can make, on average, between $40,000 and $60,000 a year. The ones who succeed are as adept at sales as they are at event planning.

"I generally work on a flat fee. How I set the fee depends on a combination of factors including knowing what it will take for me to accomplish a job, what I believe I deserve to make, what other planners in my area charge, what the averages are for the industry, what I need to make to cover expenses, and a number of other factors.

"I find that charging a percentage is unfair to the client; it's also not necessarily prudent. It may take me three to four times longer to plan a low budget event than it would to plan a high budget one. So charging the client a percentage isn't good business to me. Plus, why should it be to my advantage and against the client's benefit not to find the best prices, since the more people charge my client the more money I make?

"I only make money on jobs that are profitable to me. I am the last one paid, so unless I do my job perfectly, I might not make a lot of money on a job."

Advice from Phyllis Cambria

"While it's great to be creative and organized, I imagine that you are finding that you have stiff competition out there. Party/event planning is rapidly becoming a hot career choice. That means that more people are applying for the limited number of openings available or are trying to start a business in a market that's crowded with other planners or in an area that can't support a planner.

"Here are some suggestions how you can get to the front of that list or get your business off the ground:"

Keep Your Day Job

"This is not a business you can jump into overnight. Be prepared to work nights and weekends. If you have a "day job," you might want to keep it as you build your client base and/or experience. Many in-house planners are paid based upon experience and education, so build a strong portfolio and résumé.

"Remember, even if you were to start working on a project today, you might not actually finish the project for three to six months from now or longer. That means you don't get paid until then. You may have deposits from your client, but you need those to give deposits to the other vendors and order supplies."

Network

"You need to network with other event/party professionals whenever and wherever you can. The key to being a great planner is not only having terrific ideas and being incredibly organized, you also must know the best place to get whatever it is you need to implement your plans for your client. That means you need to read trade magazines such as *SpecialEvents* and attend various trade shows.

"You likely won't find most of your best vendors in the Yellow Pages. Why? Amazingly the best vendors we deal with often are not listed because they don't have to be. They get enough work through planners that they don't need the general consumer. That means you will often be able to offer your clients resources that they couldn't probably find for themselves.

"You also should attend trade shows and visit hotels or places where events are being planned and stop by during setup. Collect business cards from people whose work you see there. If there is a planner there, however, make sure to introduce yourself and get his or her permission first. You don't want to start out in the biz with another planner bad-mouthing you and saying your were "poaching" vendors.

"Build your Rolodex. Guard it with your life. Whenever and wherever you find someone who offers a product or service you think you could possibly use, at any time in your career, even if you don't have an immediate need, get a business card and keep in touch. People move, change phone numbers, add new products and services. If you don't stay in touch, when you need the product or service, you might not be able to find it.

"You have to remember that most vendors will only give you a minor professional discount—if any—when you are starting with them. After you have given them repeat business—and more than one or two jobs—then you can negotiate with them for bigger discounts. Up until then, you are an unknown quantity to them."

Volunteer

"Everyone always wants to know how they are going to get experience. It's easy. Volunteer! Work with other planners to get more of the day-to-day experience of running an event business, work on an event, and/or offer your services without pay to nonprofit agencies that do fund-raisers but don't have an event person on board. Think of it as great training you're not paying for except by contributing your time. This is very similar to the old apprenticeship programs from years ago.

"This does not mean that you can then turn around and steal clients from the person who helped you get experience. It means that you work as hard as you can to build your own bank of knowledge and a reputation.

"While you're building your client list, working on a charity event is a great way to showcase your work. Remember that these are often the 'ladies who lunch' and who plan all the big social charity events. These days, either they or their husbands are also involved with big corporations.

"If you do not have any experience, do not volunteer to run the event. It's entirely too easy to become overwhelmed when you're starting out. Not only will you hurt your reputation, possibly irreversibly, but it's also not fair to the charity that needs the money you should have helped them raise. Mistakes are costly in more ways than one.

"It's better to work on one or two subcommittees. If you do well and you think you would like more responsibility, then you may volunteer to run the committee for the next event. Eventually, when you have acquired a sufficient amount of knowledge and experience, you may offer to chair the entire event.

"Don't forget that you need to have a portfolio of your work to show potential clients. People aren't going to give you money just because you helped plan your sister's wedding or your friends think you do a great job with all your parties. These events will help you build your portfolio and reputation."

The Sales Aspect

"The part of this business that we all hate, but the part that we all spend the bulk of our time on is finding new business. Developing prospects, writing proposals, rewriting proposals, and convincing someone to hire us are the things we spend more time on than any other. After all, if you don't have clients, you don't have anything to be creative on.

"Generalists actually have the hardest job of finding clients. I know that sounds strange, but you have to remember that if you specialize in a type of event, you can at least focus your marketing and prospecting more productively.

"Corporate work is the most lucrative and the most difficult to get. Corporate event planners work largely by reputation and recommendation from other in-house corporate planners. These events usually have a sales component, and they must have a provable component of how successful the event was as a marketing or sales tool. That is a highly difficult specialty.

"You must remember that these people must go back to their bosses or stockholders to explain the expenditure and why it was necessary and how successful it was in achieving the goal."

5

In-House Event Planners

An in-house event planner works for a particular employer, producing events the employer needs. Working in-house allows new event planners to amass hands-on experience. In-house planners can often use their jobs as training grounds for going out on their own at a later date.

But not all planners have self-employment as a goal. Although self-employed event planners have more independence, there are some advantages to working as an in-house planner. Let's compare independent work to in-house work, looking at both the advantages and disadvantages:

Independent Planning Versus In-House Planning

Independent planners can pick and choose the events they work on. In-house planners often have no choice.

Independent planners can work on a variety of event types. In-house planners often report boredom as a problem. There is a lot of repetition, producing the same events over and over, often with the same audience or guest list. The goals of the events could be the same from event to event as well.

Independent planners often have larger budgets with which to produce the events. In-house planners, as a rule, have to find ways to stretch the dollar.

Independent planners have to look for their own clients. They can spend more time marketing their services than planning events. Sometimes independent planners spend time and energy writing proposals for events they don't get hired for. In-house planners are given assignments.

Independent planners have to cover all their business expenses, including insurance and office supplies. In-house planners have operating costs and office supplies covered by their employer.

Independent planners never know exactly how much money they'll make from month to month, year to year. In-house planners, for the most part, earn a set salary.

Basically, as an independent planner you must adjust your vision to your clients' dreams, goals, and budget. You may have to deal with a number of people who are not necessarily the decision makers, and you may have to create and re-create a proposal more than once.

In addition, as an independent you have to rely heavily on your vendors. Your first contact with them would be to get quotes for you to include in your proposals. This takes up the vendors' time, and if your proposals don't always land you the contract, you might find that the cooperation of the vendors starts to wane. There never is an unlimited supply of quality vendors. Your success can depend on your relationship with the best vendors and suppliers in the business.

Another disadvantage to going out on your own, mentioned earlier, is that it's a lot more expensive to run a business than most people realize. You have to provide every piece of equipment, every piece of paper and paper clip for yourself.

There is the potential for an independent planner to make good money, but all of that depends on both a lot of hard work and some luck. Employment with a company guarantees a paycheck, and for some, that's the bottom line.

Who Hires In-House Event Planners?

The main employers of in-house planners are:

- corporations
- event production companies
- hotels
- nonprofits
- government

Corporate In-House Planners

This is a very broad category and can cover every type of company imaginable, from publishing houses or insurance companies to medical supply firms.

As explained earlier, working as an in-house planner for a corporation has its pluses and minuses. You might work with the same clientele and the same type of event. You might have restrictions on the budget and your creativity, and you might have to answer to more people than you'd like. Event planner Dianna Bacchi lets us see what it's like working for a publishing company.

Dianna earned her B.A. in media and communications at the State University of New York College at Old Westbury in 1997. After college, she went to work as a meeting planner in the Professional Books Division of McGraw-Hill, a large publishing house in New York City. She worked for McGraw-Hill for about two years.

"I first realized I had the skills to be a professional meeting planner at my wedding. Looking back over my life, it seems I was always planning events in one form or another. I realized that I had what it took to do this sort of thing, and I actually enjoyed it.

"My first job planning events was in college. I coordinated all rush and alumni events for the sorority I was in.

"After college I first worked for McGraw-Hill in the publicity department. I created press releases and contacted reviewers for the training, careers, outdoor, and aviation titles. I also created two newsletters, *Beyond Flight* and *Training News*, which helped our books reach target publications.

"When the last position I worked in there became available, I applied for it and got it. I knew I could plan the meetings and do a good job."

The Job

"I handled every detail of the meetings for our sales division from picking the hotels, to menu selections, to reconciling and paying the bill, and a few thousand things that fell in between.

"You need to be detail-oriented to a fault, and you need to be quick on your feet and able to troubleshoot problems. For example, one time an international attendee at one of our meetings got something in his eye, and I had to find him a clinic in New York City that would take his insurance.

"My job is very broad. I plan three sales conferences a year with about 130 attendees at each. I also handle a majority of the work for BookExpo America, which is the largest trade show in publishing. To top it all off, I am the assistant to the Vice President of Sales.

"A typical day starts off with about thirty E-mails and ten voice mails, each one with a request. There is never a time when you can say 'I have done all my work.' Even after your meeting, you need to go through the bill with a fine-toothed comb. Every conference I find thousands of dollars in mistakes."

Upsides and Downsides

"The greatest thing about meeting planning is the way hotels treat you. You have the capability to spend hundreds of thousands of dollars at a hotel or convention center and these places know it. They will always treat you well because they want your business.

"The most frustrating thing about my job is that if you are a good meeting planner everyone thinks it is so easy. Most people don't see how hard you work; it is one of those things you physically have to do to know what it is really like.

"I spend countless hours outside of work thinking about every little detail, and I never enjoy the beautiful places we go. I am always on the clock, twenty-four seven."

Advice from Dianna Bacchi

"The best advice I can give anyone is know someone. And make sure you're detail oriented and a troubleshooter. Be careful before signing contracts with the hotels or other venues. I'd recommend taking a course in contract law."

Event Production Companies

Unlike corporations, for which event planning constitutes generally only a small portion of business activities, event production companies are formed for the sole purpose of planning, producing, and sometimes marketing events. Employees gear their activities toward event planning and little else. They might have to look for clients or market an upcoming event they're planning, but event planning is their primary focus, not a secondary one as with other types of corporations.

Mary Tribble, profiled in Chapter 4, is founder of Tribble Creative Group, an event production company in Charlotte, North Carolina. Here she lets us see what it's like putting on corporate events.

"In broadening our services, we have actually moved away from social events. While we still do a few weddings and bar mitzvahs, most of our work is corporate, convention, and nonprofit based. In addition to social events, we've expanded and we've also added event-marketing services, which are executed several ways. First, we help our clients market their events to their audience, whether through media, public relations, advertising, or direct mail. Second, we now have a sponsor services manager, who helps our clients secure event partners—companies and organizations that are interested in sponsoring some portion of an event.

"All types of corporations hire us—banks, insurance companies, manufacturers—you name it! We do grand openings, client celebrations, incentive weekends, sales meetings, and team building events."

Here's a description of a recent event by insurance giant Royal & SunAlliance. It typifies the bigger events the Tribble Creative Group puts on. It was the kickoff of a new values-based management initiative for an insurance company.

"As a company grows through mergers or acquisitions, communicating a message—especially a cultural one—becomes increasingly difficult," says Mary. That's what Royal & SunAlliance faced after it acquired Orion Capital Corporation, creating a megafirm. After realizing that these issues could only be solved through a change in the foundation of its business practices, it was time to roll out company-wide training to get the entire firm working and communicating on the same page. It began with one major event.

Management wanted to ensure that this new initiative would be embraced, not ignored. The solution was a multimedia two-hour presentation originating before two thousand associates in Charlotte, North Carolina, and up-linked via satellite to forty cities—and an additional five thousand associates—across the country.

To keep things interesting, the event format was created to include a mix of live speeches, panels, and video production. A special technology allowed the creation of an animated character named Dickens. Dickens was projected onto two large screens on stage and connected to an actor backstage with a computer with sensors. The character was cast as a manager who had been around Royal & SunAlliance for years and had seen all of the new management initiatives he'd ever wanted to see. Through constant interruptions and humorous interjections in conversation with the senior management team on stage, Dickens served to disarm the skeptics.

Although the five values being promoted during the event—truth, trust, teamwork, excellence, and adaptability—had depth and meaning, there was a need to create potential for inspiration.

The theme "From This Moment" was created to help illustrate new behaviors that management wanted to implement. The event began with a dramatic video production set to music with no narration, featuring Royal & SunAlliance associates displaying behaviors of the new values while the words "From This Moment: Truth," and "From This Moment: Trust," and so forth, panned across the screen.

A metaphor was also chosen to represent the needed change. The ringing of a bell was chosen to signify a universal call to action. A bell was featured in various ways during the video presentation. At the program's conclusion, as the CEO called his associates to action, a video featured all the actors ringing their bells, interspersed with dramatic photographs of bells across the world. Then, the curtain was raised and the theater doors opened as 150 Royal & SunAlliance associates poured on stage and down the aisles, ringing their bells as a call to action. Each guest received his or her own bell as a reminder and message reinforcement.

"We prefer producing events that include the challenge of communicating an important message to the intended audience," explains Mary Tribble. "Our approach with projects is very strategic. We help our clients determine their message through a process called Strategic Message Development, then help them determine the best type of event elements (i.e., video, presentation, entertainment, and so forth) to communicate that message. Any event that includes this strategic approach is a good project for us.

"We also enjoy producing events that contribute something to the community. For instance, one of our clients is a large grocery store chain that has hired us to help it produce a Thanksgiving Day event to feed the hungry and homeless. Our mission statement is 'To inspire others and affect positive change.' We try to accomplish this through all the events we produce.

"We handle all the strategic and creative development, scripting, storyboarding, administration of event logistics, registration, and related tasks. We contract out catering, technical services, decor, video production, entertainment, and other event components.

"I personally handle more of the business development end—sales, marketing, keeping out in the public eye. I have a sales director who supports me on this. I am usually involved in the creative end of an event also; then my event managers and coordinators handle all the logistics. That can be everything from keeping day-to-day client contact, running meetings, writing meeting notes, dealing with vendors, getting cost estimates, doing budgets, creating event layouts, plotting production schedules and timelines, and so forth. Now, I can afford to delegate that much because I have a staff of twelve people. When my company was smaller, I still did a lot of the hands-on work as well.

"We charge clients an hourly fee, which varies depending on the person doing the work. We have three levels of hourly fees: one for principals (my time and my partners), one for event managers, and another for event coordinators. Fees for projects can range from $5,000 to $50,000 or more, depending on the complexity of the project."

Advice from Mary Tribble

"Be willing to take an entry-level job to get the experience you need. There are many jobs in a corporation that has event planning as one component of the duties. There are many more of these than there are full-time event managers. Careers in corporate communications, corporate affairs, marketing, and meeting planning will allow you to gain some valuable experience as you move toward a full-time career in event management."

Hotel and Convention Center In-House Planners

Because hotels and convention centers are so often the venue of choice for many events—from weddings to, well, conventions—it's a logical place for event planners to seek employment. Event planners might carry a variety of job titles (see Chapter 1) and could work for the following departments:

- sales
- catering
- food and beverage
- conventions and meetings
- convention services
- banquets

A Convention Services Manager

Michelle McBain, convention services manager for a major hotel in Albuquerque, New Mexico, earned her B.S. in hotel, restaurant, and tourism management in 1999 from New Mexico State University in Las Cruces, New Mexico.

Getting Started

"I wanted to get into a field that was exciting and challenging, one in which I could meet different people and experience different situations. As part of my degree program, I did an internship with a meeting management company in Colorado Springs, Colorado. After my internship, I moved to Albuquerque and began applying for various positions at several hotels so that I could get my foot in the door. I accepted a position at a large hotel as a one-stop sales manager. I would book business and detail it as well.

"Then a former co-worker of mine, who at the time was working where I am now, informed me of the position opening in convention services and put me in contact with the director of sales. I interviewed with the director of sales and the food and beverage director and was offered the position."

The Job

"I act as a liaison between clients and the hotel staff, organizing and detailing conferences and events. I ensure that both the client and the hotel abide by the terms of the sales contract. Once the sales manager has received a definite booking agreement, the file is turned over to me and I handle all of the group's needs, from preplanning to postmeeting reporting. Preplanning involves communicating with the client on the specifics of the conference such as room setups, audiovisual requirements, exhibit setups, menus, and guest room reservations. Once I have the client's specifications for the conference, I relay this information to the hotel staff through banquet event orders and group résumés. I conduct pre-conference meetings with the client and the hotel staff.

"During the conference, I meet with the client periodically to go over the agenda for the next twenty-four hours and to ensure that expectations are being met, if not exceeded. I stay in constant communication with the hotel staff, as there are always last minute changes and requests.

"It is also my responsibility to sell more services and increase revenue from a booking. Some ways I can do this are by offering the meeting planner an upscale dessert with lunch or dinner, suggesting wine with dinner, or suggesting added breaks during the agendas.

"I detail such events as fund-raisers; local, statewide, and national conferences; seminars; workshops; trade shows; surprise parties; and other social events. One event I just completed was a continuing education conference for a national association. The group is a repeat client of several years and usually has an expected attendance of six to seven hundred people. The coordinators of this particular conference are not the most organized and are usually tardy in submitting their specifications for the meeting. I met with one of the coordinators one afternoon about two weeks prior to the conference to review audiovisual requirements, menus, and setup. The only details she did not have for me were the actual room assignments that each workshop was to take place in. This information would not be provided to me until the following week—one week before the conference. Without the room assignments, I could not prepare banquet event orders as I didn't know what audiovisual or room setup went to what room. (Keep in mind that convention service managers like to have everything completed at least two weeks prior to the conference, if not sooner.)

"I was given the room assignments six days prior to the first day of the conference. My stress levels went up, as I knew that the hotel staff was relying on me to provide the information needed to prepare labor schedules and food orders. I completed the banquet event orders within the next few days, prepared and distributed a group résumé to the various departments, and scheduled a preconference meeting that Monday prior to the start of the conference. At the preconference meeting, I welcomed the clients and introduced them to the hotel staff. Each member of our staff then introduced himself or herself to the clients. We reviewed the group résumé and asked the clients if they had any questions or concerns. At this point, one of the coordinators wanted to discuss specifics such as room setups and audiovisual requirements.

"I informed the client that we would have a separate meeting after the preconference with the banquet manager, chef, and audiovisual technician to go over those types of specifics. Note that it is important for the convention services manager to maintain control over the meeting. Otherwise, clients will rattle on about things not relevant to the discussion at hand.

"After the preconference meeting, the clients and I met with the banquet manager and audiovisual technician to discuss each banquet event order. As expected, there were several last minute changes to note. Again, it was necessary for me to control the pace of the meeting because the clients would spend too much time on each banquet event order. Finally, we had obtained all of the specifics necessary to the conference. The conference would begin the following day with registration, exhibit setups, and a preconference institute. All went smoothly the first day, and the chef received several compliments on the food he had prepared for the preconference institute.

"During the next two days of the conference, I assisted the kitchen staff for one meal function and assisted the restaurant during the lunch hour because most of the attendees were on their own for lunch.

"I would periodically meet with the clients to ensure that all was going well. The only issues they had during the entire conference was that one room was too hot and it took our engineering department a while to finally control the temperature of the room, and a few minor audiovisual malfunctions. They were very happy with the service our banquet department employees provided because they were very attentive and quickly responded to the client's needs.

"One issue that was brought to my attention by our banquet manager was that several of the speakers wanted to change the setup of their workshops at the last minute. The coordinators for the conference asked the banquet staff to honor the requests of the speakers. This involved more turns than what was originally anticipated and more labor as well. Any time there are last minute changes in a room setup, there is an additional fee charged to the client for each change. However, this time it wasn't enforced. I know now for next year to bring this particular issue to the table with the client so that all involved understand the importance of obtaining the necessary information from the speakers ahead of time. This will avoid the unnecessary stress placed on the hotel staff.

"There is always something to be learned from a conference. All in all, everything went well, and the clients were very pleased with their event.

"As part of my job, I also assist the director of catering in organizing client appreciation parties and familiarization tours. The sales and catering department hosts client appreciation parties once or twice a year to thank our most loyal clients for their continued business and support. Familiarization tours are usually hosted by the local Convention and Visitors Bureau and provide national meeting planners the opportunity to experience or familiarize themselves with the hosting city—local restaurants, entertainment venues, hotel properties, and so forth. The purpose for familiarization tours is to encourage meeting planners to book their conferences in the host city.

"Working for a hotel is very different from working for a corporation. If working for a corporation, I would have more control over my environment and my work schedule. In a hotel, every day is different. You cannot always anticipate guests' last minute requests. You don't always know in what direction you're going to be pulled. Sometimes I'm called to assist the banquet staff with a last minute turn on a room setup or to assist the kitchen staff with plating-up for a large meal function. Sometimes the accounting department needs assistance resolving a billing dispute with the client. A hotel conference planner needs to be flexible and patient in dealing with clients and hotel staff.

"My job is challenging and fun. My workday is both busy and interesting. I usually work forty-five to fifty hours per week. I have a great rapport with my co-workers and other hotel staff, which makes my job enjoyable.

"Some days can be stressful, especially when clients make last minute time changes or additions to their agenda. My typical workday involves calling clients to obtain specifications for their conferences, meeting with the chef regarding special menu requests, meeting with the catering and food and beverage directors regarding updates or changes on upcoming groups, meeting with the banquet manager regarding room setups, and working on banquet event orders and group résumés.

"The best part of my job is working with the hotel staff, organizing the event, and meeting different people. It is very satisfying when an event goes really well and the client and the attendees are happy. It is difficult and challenging when you work with inexperienced meeting planners (the clients) and they don't realize the importance of getting information to you in a timely manner. Sometimes you can do everything right on your part, but things go terribly wrong on the operational side of things."

Salaries

Michelle McBain earns $30,000 per year plus bonuses. "Someone just starting can expect to earn between $27,000 and $32,000, depending on the property and location."

Advice from Michelle McBain

"I would encourage anyone getting into this field to work an entry-level position at a hotel or meeting planning company and look for promotions within the industry. A B.S. in business is important as well as work-related experience.

"Hotel conference planners needs to be flexible, patient, friendly, outgoing, and somewhat assertive. They should also possess good problem-solving skills."

In-House Planners for Nonprofits

This category can cover everything from the Olympics or the American Cancer Association to the National Trust for Historic Preservation. Event planning for nonprofits takes on the same characteristics as for any other type of event. They are similar to corporate events in that they must have an element of financial success or media exposure. It's almost guaranteed, though, that event planners working for nonprofits will be limited in their budget because every dollar the charity spends on the event is one less that goes toward its causes.

Before becoming a party planner (see Chapter 4), Phyllis Cambria worked as an in-house event planner for a nonprofit. "One of the major advantages of working for a nonprofit as an in-house planner for almost six years was that I never had to look for work. There were always new events to take on. Although it required a lot more work on my part, because I didn't have a budget that allowed me to hire outside vendors too often, the creativity it took to create an event with little money was very rewarding. It was also very nerve-racking, because often I was juggling several events simultaneously."

Government Event Planners

Some government agencies or departments, when in need of event planning, work with outside consultants. Other departments or agencies hire full-time event planners or include event planning as part of the duties of another position. For example, public affairs or public information officers working on the federal, state, or local government level often need event planning skills to organize events as a part of their regular job.

Government events cover everything from banquets to recruitment fairs, in-house workshops, seminars, and training. One of the biggest and most obvious areas in special events would be for help organizing political campaigns. A good political campaign can be viewed as a series of events, repeated around the country. To pull this off successfully, a candidate needs an excellent team of workers, some of whom must be experienced event planners.

Campaigns consist of speeches, ribbon cutting ceremonies, awards ceremonies, and traveling back and forth through the geographic political arena. As you can see, there are a lot of logistics to handle.

Looking for work? Contact local candidates and volunteer to help with their campaigns. This is a great way to get experience—and perhaps to get offered a full-time, paying job down the road.

Sample Job Listings

Here are some sample job descriptions that will give you an idea of the type of jobs in-house event planners do. Your own search will reveal similar job listings.

Job Title: Sales Managers

Type of Organization: Hotel Group

Location: California

Position Description: We are looking for seasoned sales professionals to further revenue growth from existing accounts as well as through development of new markets.

Responsibilities include the traditional calling on accounts via phone, fax, E-mail, and written correspondence; presentations; representation at trade shows; attendance at local and regional chamber of commerce events; and, most important, the implementation of resourceful strategies and tactics to bring in incremental business.

Computer skills are necessary.

Qualifications and Experience: Two years minimum experience in sales and marketing and a two-year college degree or equivalent formal education are required. Excellent communication skills (written and verbal) are necessary. Must be able to drive a personal vehicle and must hold a valid driver's license. Knowledge and skill in sales presentation techniques is required.

Contact Information: Please submit a résumé via E-mail.

Job Title: Conference and Meetings Coordinator

Type of Organization: Professional Association

Location: Illinois

Position Description: We seek an experienced professional to serve as our Conference and Meetings Coordinator. Position responsible for oversight, direction, and coordination of all aspects of our annual conference and exhibition and our committee and board meetings. This individual will also provide coordination of anticipated future education and training sessions and other responsibilities as assigned. Working under the supervision of our Director of Marketing, the Conference and Meetings Coordinator will play an integral role in the continued enhancement and growth of our annual conference. This individual will also serve as the staff liaison to our Conference Planning Committee and to our outsourced conference consultants.

Qualifications and Experience: We require an experienced individual with excellent communication and organization skills and a strong background in meeting planning and fiscal management. Must be a self-starter; goal-oriented; able to work with a mixture of staff, volunteers, and vendors; and capable of managing multiple projects in a fast-paced association environment. Position includes some travel.

Salary: $25,000 to $34,999.

Contact Information: Explain why you are the right person for this important position in your cover letter and include your résumé and salary history.

Job Title: Program Coordinator

Type of Organization: Medical Corporation

Location: Delaware

Position Description: Temporary to permanent position to manage meetings and events from inception through final billing. Act as the liaison with pharmaceutical sales managers on budget, agenda, and attendance targets. Day-to-day responsibilities include management of the communication and registration process, booking and contracting with hotels and restaurants, speaker coordination, air travel, ground transportation, audiovisual production, food and beverage. Responsibilities will include coordination of meetings, database, invitations, attendee registration and confirmation, on-site materials, shipping, and postmeeting follow-up reconciliation.

Qualifications and Experience: Job requirements include strong interpersonal skills, a high level of customer service, and the ability to interact with clients, speakers, senior-level sales management, physicians and their office staff, and vendors. Qualities include significant attention to detail, organization, ability to multitask, patience, stamina, flexibility to adhere to change, and ability to work well under time constraints and pressure. Knowledge of the medical communications or pharmaceutical/device industry desired. Specific experience in meeting planning of medical meetings preferred. Strong background working in database environment; computer skills are necessary. Bachelor's degree or some college is preferred. Prior experience in meetings and/or hospitality industry a plus.

Salary: $25,000 to $34,999.

Contact Information: Submit résumé and cover letter via E-mail.

Additional Help

M&C magazine commissions reports every two years, covering economic activity in the meeting planning industry. It provides insights into how much money meeting planners spend on meetings, how many meetings they plan, where they bring those meetings, the nature of attendees, types of facilities preferred, factors that go into site selection, loyalty to hotel chains, and more.

Reports are available for a fee and can be ordered online at: meetings-conventions.com/contact/salesstaff.html.

6

Related Fields

Event planning is a collaborative effort. To put on successful events, planners rely on the services of vendors and on advertising, marketing, and public relations and publicity professionals.

Sometimes people working in the above mentioned fields desire a career change and move over into event planning. It can work the other way around, too. Some event planners might decide to focus on a single aspect of the industry, such as marketing or advertising. This chapter gives a bird's-eye view of related career possibilities.

Vendors

Event planners rely on the services of many types of vendors to pull off their events, including:

- caterers
- bakeries and cake decorators
- bridal shops

- floral arrangers and florists
- hotel ballrooms or other facilities
- musicians
- photographers and videographers

Experienced event planners usually maintain a card file on each vendor, keeping track of the various contracts and how well each vendor has fulfilled them. Good note-taking skills will help ensure the best selection of vendors for each event.

Advertising, Marketing, Promotions, and Public Relations

For a commercial event to be successful, event planners and their clients have to make sure they are reaching the intended audience and that they are doing so in the most effective way. Some full-service event planning firms also include advertising, marketing, promotions, and PR services along with actual event production. Advertising, marketing, promotions, public relations, and sales managers coordinate market research, marketing strategy, sales, advertising, promotion, pricing, product development, and public relations activities.

Managers oversee advertising and promotion staffs, which usually are small, except in the largest firms. In a small firm, managers may serve as a liaison between the firm and the advertising or promotion agency to which many advertising or promotional functions are contracted out. In larger firms, advertising managers oversee in-house account, creative, and media services departments. The account executive manages the account services department, assesses the need for advertising, and, in advertising agencies, maintains the accounts of clients.

The creative services department develops the subject matter and presentation of advertising. The creative director oversees the copy chief and art director and their respective staffs.

The media director oversees planning groups that select the appropriate communication media for disseminating the advertising—radio, television, newspapers, magazines, the Internet, or outdoor signs, for example.

Promotion managers supervise staffs of promotion specialists. They direct promotion programs combining advertising with purchase incentives to increase sales. In an effort to establish closer contact with purchasers—dealers, distributors, or consumers—promotion programs may involve special events or direct mail, telemarketing, television or radio advertising, catalogs, exhibits, inserts in newspapers, Internet advertisements or websites, in-store displays, or product endorsements.

Marketing managers develop the firm's detailed marketing strategy. With the help of subordinates, including product development managers and market research managers, they determine the demand for products and services offered by the firm and its competitors. In addition, they identify potential markets, for example, business firms, wholesalers, retailers, the government, or the general public. Marketing managers develop pricing strategy with an eye toward maximizing the firm's share of the market and its profits while ensuring that the firm's customers are satisfied. In collaboration with sales, product development, and other managers, they monitor trends that indicate the need for new products and services and oversee product development. Marketing managers work with advertising and promotion managers to promote the firm's products and services and to attract potential users.

Public relations managers supervise public relations specialists. These managers direct publicity programs to a targeted public. They often specialize in a specific area, such as crisis management, or in a specific industry, such as health care. They use every available communication medium in their effort to maintain the support of the specific group their organization's success depends on, such as consumers, stockholders, or the general public. For example, public relations managers may clarify or justify the firm's point of view on health or environmental issues to community or special interest groups.

Public relations managers also evaluate advertising and promotion programs for compatibility with public relations efforts and serve as the eyes and ears of top management. They observe social, economic, and political trends that might ultimately affect the firm and make recommendations to enhance the firm's image based on those trends.

Public relations managers may also confer with labor relations managers to produce internal company communications, such as newsletters about employee-management relations, and with financial managers to produce company reports. They assist company executives in drafting speeches, arranging interviews, and maintaining other forms of public contact; oversee company archives; and respond to information requests. In addition, some handle special events such as sponsorship of races, parties introducing new products, or other activities the firm supports in order to gain public attention through the press without advertising directly.

An organization's reputation, profitability, and even its continued existence can depend on the degree to which its targeted "publics" support its goals and policies. Public relations specialists serve as advocates for businesses, nonprofit associations, universities, hospitals, and other organizations, and build and maintain positive relationships with the public. As managers recognize the growing importance of good public relations to the success of their organizations, they increasingly rely on public relations specialists for advice on the strategy and policy of such programs.

Public relations specialists handle organizational functions such as special events; media, community, consumer, and governmental relations; political campaigns; interest-group representation; conflict mediation; or employee and investor relations. However, public relations is not only "telling the organization's story." Understanding the attitudes and concerns of consumers, employees, and various other groups also is a vital part of the job. To improve communications, public relations specialists establish and maintain cooperative relationships with representatives of community, consumer, employee, and public interest groups and with representatives from print and broadcast journalism.

Informing the general public, interest groups, and stockholders of an organization's policies, activities, and accomplishments is an important part of a public relations specialist's job. The work also involves keeping management aware of public attitudes and concerns of the many groups and organizations with which they must deal.

Public relations specialists prepare press releases and contact people in the media who might print or broadcast their material. Many radio or television special reports, newspaper stories, and magazine articles start at the desks of public relations specialists. Sometimes the subject is an organization and its policies towards its employees or its role in the community. Often the subject is a public issue, such as health, energy, or the environment.

Public relations specialists also arrange and conduct programs to keep up contact between organization representatives and the public. For example, they set up speaking engagements and often prepare speeches for company officials. These specialists represent employers at community projects; make film, slide, or other visual presentations at meetings and school assemblies; and plan conventions. In addition, they are responsible for preparing annual reports and writing proposals for various projects.

In government, public relations specialists—who may be called press secretaries, information officers, public affairs specialists, or communications specialists—keep the public informed about the activities of government agencies and officials. For example, public affairs specialists in the Department of State keep the public informed of travel advisories and of U.S. positions on foreign issues. A press secretary for a member of Congress keeps constituents aware of the representative's accomplishments.

In large organizations, the key public relations executive, who often is a vice president, may develop overall plans and policies with other executives. In addition, public relations departments employ public relations specialists to write, research, prepare materials, maintain contacts, and respond to inquiries.

People who handle publicity for an individual or who direct public relations for a small organization may deal with all aspects of the job. They contact people, plan and research, and prepare material for distribution. They also may handle advertising or sales promotion work to support marketing.

Sales managers direct the firm's sales program. They assign sales territories, set goals, and establish training programs for the sales representatives. Managers advise the sales representatives on ways to improve their sales performance. In large, multiproduct firms, they oversee regional and local sales managers and their staffs. Sales managers maintain contact with dealers and distributors. They analyze sales statistics gathered by their staffs to determine sales potential and inventory requirements and monitor the preferences of customers. Such information is vital to develop products and maximize profits.

Training

A wide range of educational backgrounds are suitable for entry into advertising, marketing, promotions, public relations, and sales jobs, but many employers prefer those with experience in related occupations plus a broad liberal arts background.

A bachelor's degree in sociology, psychology, literature, journalism, event planning, or philosophy, among other subjects, is acceptable. However, requirements vary, depending upon the particular job.

For marketing, sales, and promotion management positions, some employers prefer a bachelor's or master's degree in business administration, with an emphasis on marketing. Courses in business law, economics, accounting, finance, mathematics, and statistics are advantageous. In highly technical industries, such as computer and electronics manufacturing, a bachelor's degree in engineering or science, combined with a master's degree in business administration, is preferred.

For advertising management positions, some employers prefer a bachelor's degree in advertising or journalism. A course of study should include marketing, consumer behavior, market research, sales, communication methods and technology, and visual arts—for example, art history and photography.

For public relations management positions, some employers prefer a bachelor's or master's degree in public relations or journalism. The applicant's curriculum should include courses in advertising, business administration, public affairs, public speaking, political science, and creative and technical writing. A college degree combined with public relations experience, usually gained through an internship, is considered excellent preparation for public relations work; in fact, internships are becoming vital to obtaining employment.

The ability to write and speak well is essential. Many entry-level public relations specialists have a college major in public relations, journalism, advertising, or communications. Some firms seek college graduates who have worked in electronic or print journalism. Other employers seek applicants with demonstrated communications skills and training or experience in a field related to the firm's business—science, engineering, sales, or finance, for example.

Familiarity with word processing and database applications also is important for many positions. Computer skills are vital because interactive marketing, product promotion, and advertising on the Internet are increasingly common. The ability to communicate in a foreign language may open up employment opportunities in many rapidly growing niche markets around the country, especially in large cities and in areas with large Spanish-speaking populations.

Most advertising, marketing, promotions, public relations, and sales management positions are filled by promoting experienced staff or related professional or technical personnel. For example, many managers are former sales representatives, purchasing agents, buyers, product or brand specialists, advertising specialists, promotion specialists, and public relations specialists. In small firms, where the number of positions is limited, advancement to a management position usually comes slowly. In large firms, promotion may occur more quickly.

Although experience, ability, and leadership are emphasized for promotion, advancement can be accelerated by participation in management training programs conducted by many large firms. Many firms also provide their employees with continuing education opportunities, either in-house or at local colleges or universities, and encourage employee participation in seminars and conferences, often provided by professional societies. In collaboration with colleges and universities, numerous marketing and related associations sponsor national or local management training programs. Courses include brand and product management, international marketing, sales management evaluation, telemarketing and direct sales, interactive marketing, promotion, marketing communication, market research, organizational communication, and data processing systems procedures and management. Many firms pay all or part of the cost for those who successfully complete courses.

Some associations (listed in Appendix A) offer certification programs for advertising, marketing, sales, and public relations managers. Certification—a sign of competence and achievement in the field—is particularly important in a competitive job market.

Although relatively few advertising, marketing, and public relations managers currently are certified, the number of managers who seek certification is expected to grow. For example, Sales and Marketing Executives International offers a management certification program based on education and job performance. The Public Relations Society of America offers an accreditation program for public relations practitioners based on years of experience and an examination.

People interested in becoming advertising, marketing, promotions, public relations, and sales managers should be mature, creative, highly motivated, resistant to stress, flexible, and decisive. The ability to communicate persuasively, both orally and in writing, with other managers, staff, and the public is vital. These managers also need tact, good judgment, and exceptional ability to establish and maintain effective personal relationships with supervisory and professional staff members and client firms.

Because of the importance and high visibility of their jobs, advertising, marketing, promotions, public relations, and sales managers often are prime candidates for advancement to the highest ranks. Well-trained, experienced, successful managers may be promoted to higher positions in their own, or other, firms. Some become top executives. Managers with extensive experience and sufficient capital may open their own businesses.

Employment Figures and Job Outlook

Advertising, marketing, promotions, public relations, and sales managers held about 707,000 jobs in 2000. These managers were found in virtually every industry. Sales managers held almost half of the jobs; most were employed in wholesale and retail trade, manufacturing, and services industries. Marketing managers held more than one-fourth of the jobs; services and manufacturing industries employed about two-thirds of marketing managers.

Half of advertising and promotions managers worked in services industries, including advertising, computer and data processing, and engineering and management services. More than two-thirds of public relations managers were found in services industries such as educational services, management and public relations, and social services.

Public relations specialists held about 137,000 jobs in 2000. About six out of ten salaried public relations specialists worked in services industries such as management and public relations firms, membership organizations, educational institutions, health care organizations, social service agencies, and advertising agencies. Others worked for communications firms, financial institutions, and government agencies. About 8,600 public relations specialists were self-employed.

Public relations specialists are concentrated in large cities, where press services and other communications facilities are readily available and many businesses and trade associations have their headquarters. Many public relations consulting firms are in New York, Los Angeles, Chicago, and Washington, D.C., for example. There is a trend, however, toward public relations jobs being dispersed throughout the nation, closer to clients.

Advertising, marketing, promotions, public relations, and sales manager jobs are highly coveted and will be sought by other managers or highly experienced professional and technical personnel, resulting in keen competition.

Keen competition also will likely continue for entry-level public relations jobs as the number of qualified applicants is expected to exceed the number of job openings. Many people are attracted to this profession because of the high-profile nature of the work and the relative ease of entry. Opportunities should be best for college graduates who combine a degree in journalism, public relations, advertising, or another communications-related field with a public relations internship or other related work experience.

College graduates with related experience, a high level of creativity, and strong communication skills should have the best job opportunities. Those who have new media and interactive marketing skills will be particularly sought after.

Employment of advertising, marketing, promotions, public relations, and sales managers is expected to increase faster than the average for all occupations through 2010. Increasingly intense domestic and global competition in products and services offered to consumers should require greater marketing, promotional, and public relations efforts by managers.

The number of management and public relations firms may experience particularly rapid growth as businesses increasingly hire contractors for these services instead of additional full-time staff. Projected employment growth varies by industry. For example, employment of advertising, marketing, promotions, public relations, and sales managers is expected to grow much faster than average in most business services industries, such as computer and data processing, and in management and public relations firms, while little or no change is projected in manufacturing industries.

Earnings

According to the *Occupational Outlook Handbook*, recent median annual earnings stack up as follows:

marketing managers	$71,240
sales managers	$68,520
public relations managers	$54,540
advertising and promotions managers	$53,360
public relations specialists	$39,580

The middle 50 percent earned between $29,610 and $53,620, the lowest 10 percent earned less than $22,780, and the top 10 percent earned more than $70,480.

Median annual earnings in the industries employing the largest numbers of public relations specialists were:

management and public relations	$43,690
local government	$40,760
state government	$39,560
colleges and universities	$35,080

Median annual earnings in the industries employing the largest numbers of advertising and promotions managers were:

computer and data processing services	$79,970
advertising	$58,890

Median annual earnings in the industries employing the largest numbers of marketing managers were:

computer and data processing services	$85,750
advertising	$72,590
management and public relations	$70,170

Median annual earnings in the industries employing the largest numbers of sales and public relations managers were:

computer and data processing services	$86,690
professional and commercial equipment	$84,770
new and used car dealers	$80,680
hotels and motels	$42,210

Sample Job Listings

Here are some sample want ads for jobs to give you an idea of the types of positions available. Your own search will reveal similar job listings.

Job Title: Meetings Manager

Type of Organization: European Government Tourist Office

Location: Massachusetts

Position Description: Help U.S. associations, corporation meeting planners, and specialized agencies book meetings in Europe (logistical support for location identification, promotional material, and coordination with European suppliers).

Promote Europe as a meeting destination (participation at conferences, organization of sales calls, workshops). Manage U.S. client database.

Qualifications and Experience: Must have good organizational skills and be familiar with the meetings industry. Knowledge of a foreign language is a plus.

Salary: $35,000 to $45,000.

Contact Information: Résumés should be faxed or E-mailed.

Job Title: Customer Events Planner

Type of Organization: Railway

Location: Texas

Position Description: Identify, plan, coordinate, and oversee the successful execution of various marketing events—including trade show, seminar, meeting and hospitality, incentive, recognition, or celebratory functions—hosted by the railway and/or various transportation associations. Ensure that events will reinforce corporate marketing messages, strategies, and customer satisfaction efforts. Responsible for all aspects of event management including budgets, site research and inspections, contracts, notification, logistics, catering, registration, and on-site management. Coordinate and manage trade show participation, from researching trade shows and conferences in various markets and industries to managing all elements of booth design, installation, shipping, staffing, and supplies (such as incentives and giveaways). Recommend and oversee use and production of various audiovisual elements. Oversee and manage marketing presentation library to ensure the sharing and consistent use of marketing messages. Develop and write pre- and postevent briefings; create and maintain event databases to track participation and success of, as well as leads generated from, all marketing events. Work with various vendors, including hotel and conference staffs, trade show and exhibit companies, mail houses, and specialty merchandisers.

Qualifications and Experience: Must have a thorough understanding of meeting, trade show, and event planning; effective oral and written communications skills; and ability to communicate with people at all levels. Must possess exceptional organization, negotiating, problem solving, customer relations, and customer service skills; be very attentive to detail; and be an excellent project and budget manager. Also must have the ability to work alone, or as a member of a team, to respond quickly to the needs and demands of multiple projects and events, and deliver superior results under intense deadlines in a fast-paced environment. Proficiency in various computer programs and knowledge of production, including print, electronic, and audiovisual are important, as are at least three to five years of experience in meeting or event planning. A certified meeting professional designation and a bachelor's degree in a communications, marketing, or a customer service–related field is preferred.

Salary: Negotiable.

Contact Information: Send a résumé and cover letter through regular mail.

Job Title: Sales Manager

Type of Organization: Hotel and Conference Center

Location: Arizona

Position Description: We are the state's largest conference facility (encompassing thirty thousand square feet of conference space and 210 suites and minisuites).

Qualifications and Experience: Seeking an energetic, organized, and knowledgeable hotel salesperson (minimum of one year of experience is preferred).

Salary: $35,000 to $44,999, based on experience. We provide an excellent compensation and benefits package including 401 (K) health insurance, life insurance, paid holidays, and paid vacation.

We offer a great work environment and an opportunity for career growth in a team-oriented culture.

Contact Information: Fax résumé.

A Cooperative Effort

Event planners work closely with the professionals highlighted in this chapter. A good stable of vendors makes the life of event planners easier. If they know who to call, and that good vendors are just a fingertip touch away in a well-organized card file, the event is that much closer to getting planned.

Advertising, marketing, promotions, public relations, and sales personnel are also essential to the organizing of a successful event. What's the point of an event if no one knows about it? Some events require getting the word out in fast and effective ways and event planners depend on these other professionals to do that.

In more than almost any other profession, event planners do not work alone. By its nature, the field of event planning requires a team effort. And for some, nothing's more exciting than being a team player and watching the team function together well. If that describes how you work, then event planning or its related fields might be just the career for you.

Appendix A

Professional Associations

The following event planning, advertising, public relations, sales and marketing, and wedding associations are good sources of information.

Event Planning

Center for Exhibition Industry Research
2301 S. Lake Shore Dr., Ste. E1002
Chicago, IL 60616
ceir.org

International Festivals & Events Association (IFEA)
World Headquarters
2601 Eastover Terr.
Boise, ID 83706
ifea.com

International Special Events Society (ISES)
401 N. Michigan Ave.
Chicago, IL 60611-4267
ises.com

Meeting Professionals International (MPI)
International Headquarters
4455 LBJ Freeway, Ste. 1200
Dallas, TX 75244-5903
mpiweb.org

MPI Canadian Office
329 March Rd., Ste. 232, Box 11
Kanata, ON K2K 2E1
Canada

MPI European Office
P.O. Box 22
route de Grundhof
L-6315 Beaufort
Luxembourg

Advertising

American Advertising Federation
1101 Vermont Ave. NW, Ste. 500
Washington, DC 20005-6306
aaf.org

American Association of Advertising Agencies
405 Lexington Ave., 18th Fl.
New York, NY 10174-1801
aaaa.org

Association of National Advertisers
708 Third Ave.
New York, NY 10017-4270
ana.net

Point of Purchase Advertising Institute
1600 L St. NW, 10th Fl.
Washington, DC 20036
popai.com

Public Relations

International Association of Business Communicators
One Hallidie Plaza, Ste. 600
San Francisco, CA 94102

Public Relations Society of America
33 Irving Pl.
New York, NY 10003-2376
prsa.org

Sales and Marketing

American Marketing Association
311 S. Wacker Dr., Ste. 5800
Chicago, IL 60606
ama.org

National Association of Sales Professionals (NASP)
8300 N. Hayden Rd., Ste. 207
Scottsdale, AZ 85258
http://216.119.96.39/index.html

Sales and Marketing Executives International
P.O. Box 1390
Sumas, WA 98295-1390
smei.org

Weddings

Association of Bridal Consultants
200 Chestnutland Rd.
New Milford, CT 06776-2521
bridalassn.com

National Bridal Service (NBS)
3122 W. Cary St.
Richmond, VA 23221
nationalbridal.com

Weddings Beautiful Worldwide
3122 W. Cary St.
Richmond, VA 23221
weddingsbeautiful.com
nationalbride.com

APPENDIX B

Recommended Reading

THERE IS A wealth of reference material for meeting planners. The following publications are available through Meeting Professionals International (MPI), the International Festivals & Events Association (IFEA), the International Special Events Society (ISES), or online and local bookstores.

MPI Publications: mpi.com

2001 Meetings Outlook Survey.

Ball, Corbin. *Ultimate Meeting Professional's Software Guide*, 2nd ed., 1997.

Carey, Tony. *Crisis or Conference! A Planner's Pocket Guide for Organizing Conferences*, 1997.

Focus on Your Business: A Quick Pocket Guide to Starting Your Own Business.

Foster, John S., Esq. Hotel Law: *What Hoteliers Need to Know about Legal Affairs Management*, 1995.

Foster, John S., Esq. *Independent Meeting Planners & the Law*, 1995.

Foster, John S., *Meeting & Facility Contracts*, 1995.

Goldberg, James M. *Meeting Planner's Legal Handbook*, 1996.

Howe, Jonathan T., Esq. *U.S. Meetings & Taxes*, 3rd ed.

Levitan, Jack. *Proven Ways to Generate 1,000s of Hidden $$ from Your Trade Show, Conferences and Conventions*, 1994.

Lippincott, Cheryl. *Meetings: Do's, Don'ts and Donuts: The Complete Handbook for Successful Meetings*, 1994.

Professional Meeting Management: A European Handbook.

Roysner, Mark. *Convention Center Facilities Contracts*, 1998.

IFEA Publications: ifea.com

Bove, Nancy; Charles J. Metelka, Ph.D.; Steven Remington, C.F.E.; and Carolyn Williams, C.F.E. *Event Ideas for Children.*

Bridges, Mary, ed. *Money-Making Ideas for Your Event.*

Churchard, Karen C.F.E.; Bruce Erley, A.P.R., Creative Strategies Group; and Bridget Sherrill, C.F.E., Kentucky Derby Festival, Fiesta Bowl. *Marketing Your Event.*

IFEA's Managing Volunteers, by 12 IFEA Members/Leaders in Volunteer Programs.

IFEA's Official Guide to Parades, by 17 IFEA Members/Parade Industry Leaders, Valerie Lagauskas, ed.

IFEA's Official Guide to Sponsorship, by 15 IFEA Members/Leaders in Sponsorship.

Jamieson, Paul. *Fundamental Focus.*

"K" Alferio. *Media Relations: The Good, the Blah, and the Ugly.*

Martin, Eric L. *Festival & Sponsorship Legal Issues.*

Producing a Small to Midsize Festival, by 11 IFEA Members/Leaders in the Smaller Event Market.

Storey, Bruce, ed. *101 Festival Ideas (I Wish I'd Thought Of).*

ISES Publications: specialevents.com

Goldblatt, Joe, and Carol McKibben in conjunction with ISES. *Directory of Event Management*, 2001.

Silvers, Julia Rutherford. *CSEP Exam Prep Series of CD ROM Lectures.*

Publications Available Through Online or Local Bookstores

Allen, Judy. *Event Planning: The Ultimate Guide to Successful Meetings, Corporate Events, Fundraising Galas, Conferences, Conventions, Incentives and Other Special Events.* New York: John Wiley & Sons, 2000.

American Sport Education Program. *Event Management for Sports Directors.* Champaign, IL: Human Kinetics Publishers, 1995.

Bailey, Jane H., and Thomas R. Guskey. *Implementing Student-Led Conferences* (Experts on Assessment Kit). Thousand Oaks, CA: Corwin Press, 2000.

Berkley, Susan. *Speak to Influence: How to Unlock the Hidden Power of Your Voice.* Campbell Hall Press, 1999.

Biech, Elaine, and Linda Byars. *Swindling Consultant's Legal Guide.* San Fransisco: Jossey-Bass, 2000.

Boehme, Ann J. *Planning Successful Meetings and Events: A Take-Charge Assistant Book.* New York: AMACOM, 1998.

Bowes, Betty. *Life of the Party: A Guide to Building Your Party Plan Business* (Fifty-Minute Series). Menlo Park, CA: Crisp Publications, 1998.

Catherwood, Dwight W., ed., and Richard L. Van Kirk. *The Complete Guide to Special Event Management: Business Insights, Financial Advice, and Successful Strategies from Ernst & Young*. New York: John Wiley & Sons, 1992.

Clark, Beverly. *Weddings: A Celebration*. North Hollywood, CA: Wilshire Publishing, 1996.

Coons, Patti. *Gala!: The Special Event Planner for Professionals and Volunteers*. Dulles, VA: Capital Books Inc., 1999.

Covey, Stephen R. *7 Habits of Highly Effective People*. New York: Simon & Schuster, 1990.

Cowie, Colin, and Jean T. Barrett. *Weddings*. Boston: Little Brown & Company, 1998.

Craven, Robin E., and Lynn Johnson Golabowski. *The Complete Idiot's Guide to Meeting Planning*. New York: Alpha/Macmillan Books, 2001.

DeProspo, Nancy. *Affairs of the Heart: How to Start and Operate a Successful Special Event Planning Service*. Nancy Deprospo Ltd., 1993.

Dodson, Dorian. *How to Put on a Great Conference: A Straightforward, Friendly and Practical Guide*. Adolfo Street Publications, 1992.

Eyres, Patricia S. *Legal Handbook for Trainers, Speakers and Consultants*. New York: McGraw-Hill, 1998.

Freeman, Harry A., and Karen F. Smith. *Black Tie Optional: The Ultimate Guide to Planning and Producing Successful Special Events*, 1994.

Freedman, Harry A., and Karen Feldman. *The Business of Special Events: Fundraising Strategies for Changing Times*. Sarasota, FL: Pineapple Press, 1998.

Gardner, Liese, and Susan Terpening. *Art of Event Design*. Intertec/Miramar Communications, 1998.

Getz, Donald. *Event Management & Event Tourism.* Elmsford, NY: Cognizant Communication Corp., 1997.

Goldblatt, Joe. *Dollars & Events: How to Succeed in the Special Events Business.* New York: John Wiley & Sons, 1999.

Goldblatt, Joe. *Special Events: Best Practices in Modern Event Management,* 2nd ed. New York: John Wiley & Sons, 1997.

Goldblatt, Joe. *Special Events: Twenty-First Century Global Event Management,* 3rd ed. New York: John Wiley & Sons, 2001.

Goldblatt, Joe, and Kathleen S. Nelson. *The International Dictionary of Event Management: Over 3500 Administration, Coordination, Marketing, and Risk Management Terms from Around the World.* New York: John Wiley & Sons, 2001.

Gordon, Micki. *The Fundraising Manual : A Step by Step Guide to Creating the Perfect Event.* Gaithersburg, MD: Fig Press, 1997.

Graham, Stedman, Joe J. Goldblatt, and Lisa Neirotti. *The Ultimate Guide to Sports Marketing,* 2nd ed. [download: Adobe reader]. New York: McGraw-Hill, 2001.

Kring, Robin. *Party Creations, Book of Theme Event Design.* Baldwin Park, CA: Clear Creek Publishing, 1994.

Levinson, Jay Conrad (contributor), Mark S. A. Smith, and Orvel R. Wilson. *Guerrilla Trade Show Selling: New Unconventional Weapons and Tactics to Meet More People, Get More Leads, and Close More Sales.* New York: John Wiley & Sons, 1997.

Malouf, Lena. *Behind the Scenes at Special Events: Flowers, Props, and Design.* New York: John Wiley & Sons, 1999.

McBride-Mellinger, Maria. *The Perfect Wedding.* New York: HarperCollins, 1997.

Nichols, Barbara. *Professional Meeting Management.* Professional Convention, 1999.

Nonprofits' Insurance Alliance of California. *Managing Special Event Risks: 10 Steps to Safety.* Nonprofit Risk Management Center, 1997.

Pyeatt, Nancy. *The Consultant's Legal Guide and Forms.* Consultants Library, 1999.

Reyburn, Susan. *Meeting Planner's Guide to Historic Places.* National Trust Guide. New York: John Wiley & Sons, 1997.

Robbem, Deborah. *Expositions and Trade Shows.* New York: John Wiley & Sons, 1999.

Sachs, Patty. *Pick a Party: The Big Book of Party Themes and Occasions.* Minnetonka, MN: Meadowbrook Press, 1997.

Sachs, Patty, and Phyllis Cambria. *The Complete Idiot's Guide to Throwing a Great Party.* New York: Alpha Books/Macmillan, 2000.

Sage, Linda Seifer. *The Complete Bar/Bat Mitzvah Planner: An Indispensable, Money-Saving Workbook for Organizing Every Aspect of the Event—From Temple Service to Reception.* New York: St. Martin's Press, 1993.

Scannell, Edward, and John Newstrom. *Big Book of Business Games: Icebreakers, Creativity Exercises and Meeting Energizers.* New York: McGraw-Hill, 1995.

Schmader, Steven Wood, and Robert Jackson. *Special Events: Inside and Out.* Champaign, IL: Sagamore Publishing, Inc., 1997.

Shenson, Howard L. *How to Develop and Promote Successful Seminars & Workshops: The Definitive Guide to Creating and Marketing Seminars, Workshops, Classes, and Conferences.* New York: John Wiley & Sons, 1990.

Stallings, Betty, and Donna McMillion. *How to Produce Fabulous Fundraising Events: Reap Remarkable Returns with Minimal Effort.* Building Better Skills, 1999.

Torrence, Sara R. *How to Run Scientific and Technical Meetings.* Garrett Group, 1996.

Tutera, David, and Laura Morton. *A Passion for Parties: Your Guide to Elegant Entertaining,* New York: Simon & Schuster, 2001.

Warner, Diane. *Diane Warner's Big Book of Parties: Creative Party Planning for Every Occasion.* Franklin Lakes, NJ: Career Press, 1999.

Wendroff, Alan L. *Special Events: Proven Strategies for Nonprofit Fund Raising.* New York: John Wiley & Sons, 1999.

Wigger, G. Eugene. *Themes, Dreams, and Schemes: Banquet Menu Ideas, Concepts, and Thematic Experiences.* New York: John Wiley & Sons, 1997.

Magazines

FESTIVALS: The How-To of Festivals & Events. A publication of the International Festivals & Events Association. Available at ifea.com.

M&C magazine (Meetings & Conventions). Available through meetings-conventions.com.

The Meeting Professional Magazine. A publication of Meeting Professionals International. Available at mpi.com.

Special Events Magazine. A publication of the International Special Events Society. Available at specialevents.com.

Appendix C

University Programs

FOLLOWING ARE THE addresses of the university programs featured in Chapter 2. Undoubtedly, additional universities will start offering more programs as time goes by. Please check the Internet or any guidebook to undergraduate and graduate programs. The individual professional associations should also be able to point you in the direction of any new programs. Their addresses are provided in Appendix A.

The George Washington University
The Event Management Certificate Program
Department of Tourism and Hospitality Management
600 Twenty-First St. NW
Washington, DC 20052
gwutourism.org/main.html

Purdue University
Restaurant Hotel Institutional and Tourism Management Program
Hospitality & Tourism Management Department
Stone Hall
West Lafayette, IN 47906
cfs.purdue.edu/rhit

University of Illinois at Urbana-Champaign
Department of Leisure Studies
104 Huff Hall
1206 S. Fourth St.
Champaign, IL 61820
leisurestudies.uiuc.edu

University of Minnesota Extension Service
Certified Festival Management Program
Tourism Center
120 BioAgEng Bldg.
1390 Eckles Ave.
St. Paul, MN 55108-6040
tourism.umn.edu

University of Nevada at Las Vegas
Tourism & Convention Department
Harrah College of Hotel Administration
4505 Maryland Pkwy.
P.O. Box 456023
Las Vegas, NV 89154-6023
unlv.edu/tourism

Event Planning Association Local Chapters

IN ADDITION TO its national headquarters, each professional association listed in this appendix maintains local chapters. Below you'll find a list of local chapters that you can contact using the organization's main contact information. Current telephone numbers, board members, and E-mail addresses are listed at each organization's website. Some local chapters have websites and those are listed when available, but many chapters, especially those outside the United States, do not.

International Special Events Society (ISES)

ISES Headquarters
401 N. Michigan Ave.
Chicago, IL 60611
(312) 321-6853, (800) 688-4737
Fax: (312) 673-6953
ises.com

North America Chapters

California—Los Angeles, San Diego, Northern
  California
Central Florida, South Florida
Colorado—Denver
Georgia—Atlanta
Illinois—Chicago
Indiana
Minnesota—Minneapolis, St. Paul
Missouri
Nevada—Las Vegas
New Jersey—Mendham, Englewood, Princeton
New York—New York City, Syracuse
North Carolina—Charlotte, Raleigh, Durham,
  Chapel Hill
Ohio—Cincinnati, Columbus, Toledo
Pennsylvania—Philadelphia
Texas—Austin, Dallas, San Antonio, Houston
Virginia—Hampton Roads
Washington, DC

Canada

Toronto, Ontario

International Chapters

Australia—Melbourne, Sydney
South Africa—Johannesburg
Trinidad and Tobago
United Kingdom—London

Meeting Professionals International (MPI)

MPI International Headquarters
4455 LBJ Freeway, Ste. 1200
Dallas, TX 75244
(972) 702-3000
mpiweb.org

European Office
Route de Grundhof, 22
L-6315 Beaufort
Grand Duchy of Luxembourg
352-26876141

Canadian Office
329 March Rd., Ste. 232, Box 11
Kanata, Ontario K2K 2E1
Canada
(613) 271-8901
Fax: (613) 599-7027

United States

Arizona—Phoenix
California—San Francisco, San Diego, Orange,
 Los Angeles
Colorado—Denver
Connecticut—Stamford, Hartford
District of Columbia
Florida—Jacksonville, Miami, Tampa, Orlando
Georgia—Atlanta
Hawaii—Honolulu

Illinois—Chicago
Indiana—Indianapolis
Kansas—Kansas City
Kentucky—Louisville
Louisiana—New Orleans
Massachusetts—Boston
Michigan—Holly
Minnesota—Minneapolis
Missouri—St. Louis
New Jersey—Woodbridge
New Mexico—Albuquerque
New York—New York City, Buffalo
North Carolina—Raleigh
Ohio—West Chester
Oklahoma—Tulsa
Oregon—Portland
Pennsylvania—Philadelphia, Pittsburgh
Tennessee—Nashville
Texas—Dallas, Fort Worth, Houston, Austin
Utah—Snowbird
Virginia—Richmond
Washington—Seattle
Wisconsin—Wisconsin Rapids

Canada

Alberta—Edmonton, Calgary
British Columbia—Vancouver
Manitoba—Winnipeg
Ontario—Toronto, Ottawa
Quebec—Montreal

Central/South America

Brazil—São Paulo
Mexico—Mexico City

Europe

Belgium—Brussels
Denmark—Copenhagen
France—Paris
Germany—Munich
Italy—Rome
Norway—Oslo
Sweden—Malmo
The Netherlands—Amsterdam
United Kingdom—London

Asia

Japan—Tokyo

International Festivals & Events Association (IFEA)

ifea.com

Alabama

Alabama/Mississippi Festivals & Events Association
Foley Convention & Visitors Bureau
P.O. Box 448
Foley, AL 36536
(334) 943-1200
Fax: (334) 943-1222

Arizona

Arizona Festivals & Events Association
Arizona State University West
Rec. & Tourism Manager Dept.
P.O. Box 37100
Phoenix, AZ 85069
(602) 543-6620
Fax: (602) 543-6612

California

CalFest
(CA & NV)
Valley Decorating Company
2829 E. Hamilton Ave.
Fresno, CA 93721-3208
(559) 495-1100
Fax: (888) 495-1195
P.O. Box 7547
Tahoe City, CA 96145
(530) 583-5605
Fax: (530) 581-5101

Colorado

Colorado Festivals & Events Association
EVENTTech, Inc.
2974 W. Long Circle
Littleton, CO 80120
(303) 707-0887
Fax: (303) 707-0860
coloradofestival.com

Connecticut

Yankee Festivals & Events Association
(CT, ME, MA, NH, VT, & RI)
Burlington Parks & Rec. Dept.
645 Pine St., Ste. B
Burlington, VT 05401
(802) 865-7552
Fax: (802) 862-8027

Delaware

Mid-Atlantic Festivals & Events Association
(PA, NJ, & DE)
Sunoco Welcome America!
100 S. Broad St., Ste. 1525
Philadelphia, PA 19110
(215) 683-2202
Fax: (215) 683-2209
mafea.org

Florida

IFEA Florida
Daytona Beach Area CVB
P.O. Box 910
Daytona Beach, FL 32115
(800) 544-0415, ext. 117
Fax: (386) 255-5478
florida@ifea.com

Georgia

Georgia Festivals & Events Association
Mad Booking
83 Walton St., 3rd Fl.
Atlanta, GA 30303
(404) 215-3248
Fax: (404) 215-3249
gfea.com

Hawaii

Hawaii Festivals & Events Association
Production Hawaii, Inc.
1717 Republican St.
Honolulu, HI 96819
(808) 832-7878
Fax: (808) 832-9821

Idaho

Rocky Mountain Festivals & Events Association
(ID, MT, UT, & WY)
Utah Arts Festival
331 W. Pierpont Ave.
Salt Lake City, UT 84101
(801) 322-2428
Fax: (801) 363-8681
artsfest@xmission.com
rmfea.com

Illinois

Illinois Special Events Network
City of Rockford
5411 E. State St., #345
Rockford, IL 61108
(815) 987-5546
Fax: (815) 967-6949

Iowa

Midwest Festivals & Events Association
(KS, MO, IA, NE, & SD)
Kansas City Blues & Jazz Festival
4200 Pennsylvania Ave., Ste. 230
Kansas City, MO 64111
(816) 753-3378
Fax: (816) 531-2583

Kansas

Midwest Festivals & Events Association
(KS, MO, IA, NE, & SD)
Kansas City Blues & Jazz Festival
4200 Pennsylvania Ave., Ste. 230
Kansas City, MO 64111
(816) 753-3378
Fax: (816) 531-2583

Kentucky

Kentucky Festivals & Events Association
Kingdom Swappin' Meetin'
700 College Rd.
Cumberland, KY 40823
(606) 589-2145
Fax: (606) 589-2275

Louisiana

Louisiana Festivals & Events Association
French Quarter Festivals, Inc.
100 Conti St.
New Orleans, LA 70130
(504) 522-5730
Fax: (504) 522-5711
info@frenchquarterfestivals.org

Maine

Yankee Festivals & Events Association
(CT, ME, MA, NH, VT, & RI)
Burlington Parks & Rec. Dept.
645 Pine St., Ste. B
Burlington, VT 05401
(802) 865-7552
Fax: (802) 862-8027

Maryland

Chesapeake Region Festivals & Events Association
(MD, DC, & WV)
The High Road, Inc.
P.O. Box 5256
Springfield, VA 22150-5256
(703) 923-0800
Fax: (703) 923-0907
hyroad@aol.com

Massachusetts

Yankee Festivals & Events Association
(CT, ME, MA, NH, VT, & RI)
Burlington Parks & Rec. Dept.
645 Pine St., Ste. B
Burlington, VT 05401
(802) 865-7552

Mississippi

Alabama/Mississippi Festivals & Events Association
Foley Convention & Visitors Bureau
P.O. Box 448
Foley, AL 36536
(334) 943-1200
Fax: (334) 943-1222

Missouri

Midwest Festivals & Events Association
(KS, MO, IA, NE, & SD)
Kansas City Blues & Jazz Festival
4200 Pennsylvania Ave., Ste. 230
Kansas City, MO 64111
(816) 753-3378
Fax: (816) 531-2583

Montana

Rocky Mountain Festivals & Events Association
(ID, MT, UT, & WY)
Utah Arts Festival
331 W. Pierpont Ave.
Salt Lake City, UT 84101
(801) 322-2428
Fax: (801) 363-8681
artsfest@xmission.com
rmfea.com

Nebraska

Midwest Festivals & Events Association
(KS, MO, IA, NE, & SD)
Kansas City Blues & Jazz Festival
4200 Pennsylvania Ave., Ste. 230
Kansas City, MO 64111
(816) 753-3378
Fax: (816) 531-2583

Nevada

CalFest
(CA & NV)
Valley Decorating Company
2829 E. Hamilton Ave.
Fresno, CA 93721-3208
(559) 495-1100
Fax: (888) 495-1195

P.O. Box 7547
Tahoe City, CA 96145
(530) 583-5605
Fax: (530) 581-5101

New Hampshire

Yankee Festivals & Events Association
(CT, ME, MA, NH, VT, & RI)
Burlington Parks & Rec. Dept.
645 Pine St., Ste. B
Burlington, VT 05401
(802) 865-7552
Fax: (802) 862-8027

New Jersey

Mid-Atlantic Festivals & Events Association
(PA, NJ, & DE)
Sunoco Welcome America!
100 S. Broad St., Ste. 1525
Philadelphia, PA 19110
(215) 683-2202
Fax: (215) 683-2209
mafea.org

New Mexico

Texas Festivals & Events Association
(TX & NM)
Fiesta Oyster Bake
One Camino Santa Maria
San Antonio, TX 78228
(210) 436-3324
Fax: (210) 431-6864

New York

New York Festivals & Events Association
Seneca Lake Whale Watch
P.O. Box 226
Geneva, NY 14456
(315) 781-0820
Fax: (315) 781-2766

North Dakota

North Dakota Festivals & Events Association
Christmas Bazaar
701 Main Ave.
Fargo, ND 58103
(701) 241-8160

Oklahoma

Festivals & Events Association of Oklahoma
City of Tulsa Parks & Rec. Dept.
707 S. Houston, Ste. 200
Tulsa, OK 74127
(918) 596-2473
Fax: (918) 699-3096
feao.org

Oregon

Oregon Festivals & Events Association
University of Oregon/Management Certificate Program
2225 Washington St.
Eugene, OR 97405
(541) 345-2837
ofea@mindspring.com

Pennsylvania

Mid-Atlantic Festivals & Events Association
(PA, NJ, & DE)
Sunoco Welcome America!
100 S. Broad St., Ste. 1525
Philadelphia, PA 19110
(215) 683-2202
Fax: (215) 683-2209
mafea.org

Rhode Island

Yankee Festivals & Events Association
(CT, ME, MA, NH, VT, & RI)
Burlington Parks & Rec. Dept.
645 Pine St., Ste. B
Burlington, VT 05401
(802) 865-7552
Fax: (802) 862-8027

South Dakota

Midwest Festivals & Events Association
(KS, MO, IA, NE, & SD)
Kansas City Blues & Jazz Festival
4200 Pennsylvania Ave., Ste. 230
Kansas City, MO 64111
(816) 753-3378
Fax: (816) 531-2583

Tennessee

Tennessee Festivals & Events Association
CityScape/Fall FunFest
10 W. Broad St., Ste. 302
Cookeville, TN 38501
(931) 528-4612
Fax: (931) 525-1109
cityscape@multipro.com
tnfea.org

Texas

Texas Festivals & Events Association
(TX & NM)
Fiesta Oyster Bake
One Camino Santa Maria
San Antonio, TX 78228
(210) 436-3324
Fax: (210) 431-6864

Utah

Rocky Mountain Festivals & Events Association
(ID, MT, UT, & WY)
Utah Arts Festival
331 W. Pierpont Ave.
Salt Lake City, UT 84101
(801) 322-2428
Fax: (801) 363-8681
artsfest@xmission.com
rmfea.com

Vermont

Yankee Festivals & Events Association
(CT, ME, MA, NH, VT, & RI)
Burlington Parks & Rec. Dept.
645 Pine St., Ste. B
Burlington, VT 05401
(802) 865-7552
Fax: (802) 862-8027

Virginia

Virginia Festivals & Events Association
Historic Manassas, Inc.
9431 West St.
Manassas, VA 20110
(703) 361-6599
Fax: (703) 361-6942
vfea.org

Washington

Washington Festivals & Events Association
Issaquah Salmon Days Festival
155 NW Gilman Blvd.
Issaquah, WA 98027
(425) 392-0661
Fax: (425) 392-8101
wfea.org
wfea@mindspring.com

Washington, DC

Chesapeake Region Festivals & Events Association
(MD, DC, & WV)
The High Road, Inc.
P.O. Box 5256
Springfield, VA 22150-5256
(703) 923-0800
Fax: (703) 923-0907
hyroad@aol.com

West Virginia

Chesapeake Region Festivals & Events Association
(MD, DC, & WV)
The High Road, Inc.
P.O. Box 5256
Springfield, VA 22150-5256
(703) 923-0800
Fax: (703) 923-0907
hyroad@aol.com

Wisconsin

Wisconsin Festivals & Events Association
Summerfest
200 N. Harbor Dr.
Milwaukee, WI 53202
(414) 273-2680
Fax: (414) 287-4495
wfea.com

Wyoming

Rocky Mountain Festivals & Events Association
(ID, MT, UT, & WY)
Utah Arts Festival
331 W. Pierpont Ave.
Salt Lake City, UT 84101
(801) 322-2428
Fax: (801) 363-8681
artsfest@xmission.com
rmfea.com

Affiliated International Chapters

International Festivals & Events Association Europe
Netherlands Board of Tourism (NBT)
Post Box 458
Leidschendam
2260 MG Netherlands
31-70-3705296
Fax: 31-70-3201654
ifeaeurope.com

International Festivals & Events Association Australia
The District Council of Mount Barker
P.O. Box 54
Mount Barker
South Australia
5251 Australia
61-8-8391-1633
Fax: 61-8-8391-2064

International Festivals & Events Association Singapore
Gwyndara International
118 C Newton Rd.
Singapore 307982
Fax: 65-253-5881
gwyndara@pacific.net.sg

International Festivals & Events Association South Africa
P.O. Box 9093
Eden Glen 1613
Guateng
South Africa

ABOUT THE AUTHOR

BLYTHE CAMENSON is a full-time writer with more than four dozen books and numerous articles to her credit. Her books cover career, writing, and getting published topics. She is co-author of *Your Novel Proposal: From Creation to Contract* (Writer's Digest Books) and the author of *Careers in Writing* (McGraw-Hill/Contemporary Books).

As director of Fiction Writer's Connection (FWC), a membership organization for new writers, she teaches members how to improve their writing and how to get published. She offers E-mail courses in query-letter and book proposal writing and provides free consultation and critiquing to members. She works with both fiction and nonfiction writers. Visit her website at fictionwriters.com or contact her at bcamenson@aol.com.